Go Ye Into All the World

Faith and Engagement

Ian S. Markham

Edited By Shireen R. Baker

Black and White Edition

Copyright page

Copyright © 2011 by Ian S. Markham

First Published in the United States by:

VTS Press
3737 Seminary Rd.
Alexandria, VA 22304
www.vts.edu

Edited by
Shireen Baker

Cover Design by
Thomas Zdancewicz

ISBN 9780615504346
0615504345
Printed in the United States of America
Publication date May 2011
First Edition

To the Virginia Theological Seminary Community

Contents

Acknowledgements — vii

Forward — ix

Sermons

Chapter 1: Staying in Conversation — 3

Chapter 2: Reflections on 2009 General Convention — 8

Chapter 3: Sermon on the Theme of Citizenship — 13

Chapter 4: After the Fire — 16

Chapter 5: Out of the Ashes — 20

Chapter 6: Faith and Doubt — 24

Engagement

Chapter 7: Neither Conservative nor Liberal — 29

Chapter 8: Open Orthodoxy and Same Sex Marriage — 53

Chapter 9: Learning from Radical Orthodoxy — 70

Chapter 10: Spirituality Meets Civic Engagement — 88

Chapter 11: Conversing with Islam — 100

Chapter 12: Is Greed so Bad? — 105

Chapter 13: Seeing Through Faith — 107

Chapter 14: Richard Burridge's Jesus   110

Chapter 15: Did Bush Cooperate with Terrorists?   118

Postscript   123

Acknowledgements

Ian Markham would like to thank:

Zion's Herald, The Scottish Journal of Theology and Implicit Religion for the permission to reproduce articles from their publications.

The Betjeman Society for the use of part of the poem 'Christmas'.

The author would also like to express his gratitude both on the home front and the work front. On the home front, my wife Lesley is a star and my son Luke is fabulous. For their toleration of my long hours, I am deeply grateful. And on the work front, I am grateful to the entire Seminary community, and especially to Ms. Catric Whaley and Ms. Katie Glover.

The editor would like to thank Dean Markham for the opportunity to work on this project with him. I would also like to thank my mom and dad for all of their love and support.

Forward

It is with some hesitation that I offer this collection of sermons and essays up for publication. Sermons are, by definition, the proclaimed Word offered in a particular time to a particular place. A good sermon is written for a particular congregation. In addition, it is an oral event. Hearing is different from reading. A good sermon is not supposed to be a good article.

To mitigate these objections, I have attempted to provide a brief description of the context of each sermon. These are sermons that spoke to a significant moment. How does a thoughtful congregation cope with doubt? How does a Seminary community cope with the loss of sacred space? Therefore the introduction to each sermon is important.

Most of the essays have appeared elsewhere. So they are collected together here to provide ease of access. They all speak to the theme of engagement. How does the Church relate to an increasingly secular society? What should be the Christian view on same-sex marriage? This work of engagement is central to my vocation. The Church needs to be a constructive conversation facilitator and contributor to the major questions and issues of our day. The Christian tradition, at its best, has always seen this work of engagement as central to the Church's vocation. How we relate to the culture wars, the emergence of an aggressive secularism, and to Islam are important issues. This book is an invitation to join a conversation and to model a conversation. The essays take positions; the reader is invited to disagree. The hope is that it extends the conversation by provoking a response or a different perspective.

Selection in a book like this is always tricky. The essays are intended as illustrative of methodology and thought provoking. My only nervousness is that the only piece I have on Islam is a critical reflection on an Islamist from Pakistan. Elsewhere I have written extensively and affectionately about Islam.[1] There are so many contributors who highlight forms of Islam which are challenging for modernity and the west that I hesitate to add to that literature. So I do ask that anyone especially interested in Islam read beyond this piece to discover the richness of that remarkable tradition.

Finally, a busy Dean and President has limited time to bring such projects together. I am deeply grateful to my hardworking Dean's Assistant, Shireen Baker (junior from the Diocese of Los Angeles) who is the editor of this collection.

Ian S. Markham

---

[1] See for example Ian S. Markham, *Engaging with Bediuzzaman Said Nursi*, (Aldershot, UK: Ashgate Publishing 2009)

Sermons

Chapter 1

Staying in Conversation

This Sermon was Preached at Good Shepherd Church in Burke Virginia on August 10, 2008. It was Anglican Communion Sunday and I was the visiting preacher. The goal here was to set out the importance of the Anglican Communion for the American Church.

"I ask not only on behalf of these, but also on behalf of those who will believe in me through their word, that they may all be one."

I am sure you are familiar with the old joke (one of those moveable feasts that can be applied to all sorts of different groups) so let us pick two fundamentalist pastors. They are shipwrecked on a deserted island. Several years later they are rescued. As the rescue party lands, they discover that there are two churches on this island – one at either end. And both pastors are claiming to have founded a new international ministry.

Courtesy of Susan Shillinglaw

As with all humor, this gets to an important point. We disagree with each other with ease. We move fairly rapidly to a point of principle that makes it essential for us to walk apart. We find living with disagreement difficult. There is almost something rather enjoyable about disagreeing and the appropriate almost 'righteous' indignation we feel. The temptation to give up on the struggle of conversation across a divide where we are sure the other is wrong is often overwhelming. The history of the Christian Church is a testimony to the ease with which we disagree and divide. It is easier than staying in conversation.

Here we are on Anglican Communion Sunday. For many Episcopalians, the Communion is an exhausting, rather embarrassing entity. In 1776, Americans learned that foreigners are not entitled to interfere in the affairs of America, and yet, the Communion seems to spend all its time interfering in the American Church. There are many Episcopalians who feel that this is an outmoded entity. I want to suggest this morning that the Communion is an important reality for a whole host of reasons.

First, Americans played an important role in creating the Anglican Communion and were the prime movers behind the first Lambeth. The argument that made the Communion important was this: while the Episcopal Church might be small in the American church market, the Anglican Church worldwide is large. And this is true. Worldwide Anglicans are the third largest denomination in Christendom (after the Roman Catholics and the Orthodox churches, the Anglicans come in third with 80 plus million). Americans wanted this link – they wanted to illustrate that Anglicanism was avoiding the extremes of Geneva and Rome and returning to the purer theology of the early church. And in the early church, the bishops would meet from time to time. So the Americans persuaded the Archbishop in 1867 to convene the first Lambeth conference.

Second, being part of an international family makes us sensitive to the different demands facing the family. It is commonplace to distinguish between Muslim-majority provinces and secular-majority provinces. The Muslim majority provinces cannot afford for Anglicanism to be linked with an affirmation of homosexuality; the secular majority provinces need to reach out and provide a pastoral ministry to everyone regardless of sexual orientation. One discovery at Lambeth 2008 was that these cultural differences are every bit as important as Scripture in understanding the depth of feeling on both sides of the debate.

Third, with mobility around the globe on an increase, Anglicans need the familiar as they move from country to country. I have sung 'All things bright and beautiful' in India – suddenly connected to a people in a shared liturgy.

The Episcopal Church in the United States must continue to struggle with the Anglican Communion. We need conservative voices to keep us faithful to revelation of God in Christ; and we should be willing to spend time explaining and interpreting from the vantage point of the Eternal Word disclosed in Christ why we take the positions we do.

At this point it might be objected that this is another rant for the God of inclusivity. Surely there must be boundaries? We don't want to say that the unrepentant Nazi deserves affirmation and inclusion in this congregation.

This is a good question. And our readings today are part of the response. The author of Ephesians (sadly probably not Paul) sets out the basics. We share a faith in our Lord Jesus, one baptism, and one Creator God; these convictions are the basis of our unity. When we

Courtesy of Shireen Baker

reaffirm our faith in the Nicene Creed, we reaffirm our faith in the Trinity and in the disclosure of the Eternal Word in the life, death, and resurrection of Jesus (it is interesting how most of the creed tells us the story of that life.) This creed captures the basis for unity that we are called to live within – and note how it doesn't mention sexuality or even a view of Scripture. Living within the framework of the creed is the basis of our unity. So, there is a boundary for this inclusion; we do build on these basics.

So turning now to the Gospel, when Jesus prays to the Father that "we all might be one", what does this mean? Being one does not mean being in agreement about everything. Disagreements are inevitable. They occur in a marriage, in a congregation, in an office, and in a nation. They occur because we are human – seeing things from different vantage points, weighing the factors in different ways. God – in creation – has made it inevitable that we are going to disagree about issues. So, it cannot mean complete agreement at all times.

No instead – when Paul addresses the Church of Corinth – he captures the meaning of Jesus' request for 'us to be one' by exhorting us to be united in our disagreement. Grounded in our Nicene Creed basics, we live together with a thousand and one disagreements. It is an important witness we need to provide the world. So many parts of the world demonstrate the tragic consequences of people unable to live with disagreement as principle expresses itself in sectarian violence. We need to witness to the possibility of living together with disagreement. We need to demonstrate a capacity to converse while thinking the other is mistaken. We need to show that we can transcend schism and division.

Another objection might arise. Sometimes disagreements take the form of violence or force. Sometimes separation is a necessary strategy for survival.

This is true. But the goal for the Christian is to invite the peace of the Lord to make a difference. The moment of the peace is a crucial liturgical moment. It is not the seventh inning stretch. Learning to live with disagreement is also learning to live with the peace of the Lord. There is a real beauty in this moment. Not only are we supposed to use the moment to reflect on all those who are driving us crazy at the office – indeed recommit to seeking to bring peace to that relationship; but in the symbolic moment of shaking the hand of someone near you, you reach out to all those you are disagreeing with – feel hurt by – were damaged by - in the past. We invite those moments of past hurt to no longer damage us or hurt us. We invite the peace of the Lord to bring healing to that past. We move on – in unity with those who are different, who have hurt us, with whom we strongly disagree.

One last joke: St. Peter is showing a new arrival to heaven around. "Here are those who love art," he says pointing to a group of painters. "There are the philosophers; over there are some of the musicians. In the distance you can see those enjoying golf." Meanwhile our new arrival noticed that as St. Peter was walking around there was a rather big building at the edge of heaven. "What is that building for?" our new arrival asked. "Oh that," said St. Peter, "that is where we put the Baptists – they like to think they are the only ones here."

Being one is an anticipation of heaven. Being one is our small response to the prayer of Jesus. Being one brings healing to the pain and hurt that damaged human relationships can cause. Being one is the purpose of the Communion. Being one is the hard work of the Communion.

Lessons for the day:
John 17: 6, 15-23
Ephesians 4: 1-6

Chapter 2

Reflecting on the 2009 General Convention

The General Convention of 2009 was controversial. It had decided to allow the possibility of another bishop in a same-sex relationship to be elected. News of this had reached St. Paul's Alexandria. This congregation was deeply divided over this issue. This sermon was preached to explain the debates at General Convention.

Let us look again at the reading from Ephesians:

'Then you are no longer strangers and aliens, but you are citizens with the saints and also members of the household of God, built upon the foundation of the apostles and prophets, with Christ Jesus himself as the cornerstone. In him the whole structure is joined together and grows into a holy temple in the Lord; in whom you also are built together spiritually into a dwelling place for God.'

So, there I was sitting on the Tower of Terror at Disneyland in Anaheim, California. Naturally, this is part of my work at the General Convention of the Episcopal Church. So for those unfamiliar with the ride: the theme is the Twilight Zone; and there we are reliving the moment when the hotel became an intersection between the living and the dead (especially, for some reason, the service elevators). So, once inside the service elevator - you are suddenly dropped and then taken up again only to be dropped again. Up down, up down, up down and finally you step out and leave the hotel.

Attending the General Convention is a little like the Tower of Terror. On the upside - there are 800 deputies and 200 plus Bishops (making it one of the largest parliaments in the world); there are lots of people who care a great deal about the Episcopal Church; there are thoughtful debates and passionate worship. On the downside, there is a self-preoccupation and there are lots of hurt feelings and high emotions (on every side of the debate). For me, it was definitely a mixture of admiration and concern - a Tower of Terror ride.

Here the author of Ephesians captures the nature of the Church. We are not 'strangers and aliens,' but citizens in the best of company - the saints - building on the best foundation - the work of the apostles and prophets - and with Jesus himself as the first building block. It sounds great - we are a structure building into a holy temple.

Yet as the early church knew all too well, this building project can still be messy. We have the structure, but the basic shape is constantly shifting and moving. The total message of Ephesians is that God will succeed, sometimes despite us rather than thanks to us.

So let us return to our own embodiment of the Ephesians visions. Let us look again at our General Convention. Broadly there were three groups at General Convention; each group with its own narrative. Group one, we can call the progressives. These are men and women who are committed to the justice cause of the full inclusion of gays and lesbians. Given what we know about orientation, they argue, it is exhausting for these men and women to be second class citizens in our society and in our church. The Biblical witness, they point out, is harsher on divorce and remarriage (which the Church has rightly accepted) than on the condemnation of gays and lesbians. From this perspective, the difficult texts can be understood as follows. The rather odd story of Sodom and Gomorrah should be read as a condemnation of homosexual rape, which everyone agrees is wrong.

The Holiness code in Leviticus is an exhortation to be different from those around us, which for our Jewish forbears included not wearing clothes with mixed fibers, and for us it will be different expectations.

And Paul in Romans, one is right to condemn experiential homosexual intimacy in a vice list that includes rebellious children. But none of these passages are discussing a committed couple who know where their deepest feelings are and just need to be together. The Episcopal Church delivered on the three stipulations of the Windsor Report (we apologized; we provided a moratorium on openly gay bishops and we didn't develop any approved rites for same-sex blessings) but this didn't stop the cross-border incursions. Two of our most historic churches just miles away from St. Paul's are now under the supervision of Nigeria. For this group, we just need to do what is right and accept the consequences, which can't be much worse than the consequences with which we are already struggling.

The second group, let us call the non-separating evangelicals, has a different narrative. They really want to stay in the Episcopal Church. They worry about Scripture and the relationships with the worldwide Anglican Church. They want to be in a denomination that connects the theological dots and are really confident that our purpose for being is to seek to discern the will of God. For this group, to change the definition of marriage is major. They are working hard to stay inside the Episcopal Church and, perhaps more importantly, are trying to keep others inside the Episcopal Church. They need the breathing space. They need the conversation to continue. They need to know that their voice is welcomed. They needed the progressives to understand their predicament and pain. They fear that the hard theological work is not being done: and that we are now dissolving into an unthinking, liberal, sect that worries only about inclusion but not about God.

Courtesy of Susan Shillinglaw

The third group, let us call it the big picture group, feels that this might be a moment analogous to 'eating meat offered to idols.' Paul told the Corinthians that it is okay to eat meat offered to idols, but for the sake of the 'weaker brother' one might forego this entitlement. This is a group that knows the mind of the Church is made up. This group supports the justice issue. But this group feels that for the sake of relationship, for the sake of friendship, for the sake of remaining connected with conservatives, we should allow both culture and the church some time to adjust. This is a group that admires the Windsor Report for keeping lay and priest sexuality off the radar and that the only restriction was the expectation around the Bishops. Given Bishops in the Episcopal Church make determinations on the appropriate circumstances for remarriage, it does sound odd when that person is technically cohabiting. For this group, three more years of being Windsor observant would have been wise.

The Tower of Terror ride felt different for each group. At different times during the convention, different groups were up and down. Initially it was the progressives that worried: the house of Bishops was sending clear signals that they were disinclined to change the moratorium on openly gay bishops; the third group was pleased and relieved. Then the mood of the Convention changed. And the first group – the progressives - moved up and the second and third groups – the conservatives and big picture groups - found themselves falling.

The decisions are now well known. But for those who missed them: we are open to receiving an openly gay Bishop as a nomination from a diocese and we are starting work on 'same-sex' marriage rites to be considered at the next General Convention. So where does that leave us?

First, it leaves us where we have always been. Like Jesus in the Gospel, we are still in the business of service and care; feeding the sick, preaching the Gospel, and bringing the sacraments to the people. General Conventions come and go; our worship here is a constant stabilizing reality. Second, it leaves us in a church which is messy and complicated. But that is OK too. It has always been the case - just get use to it. God brings about the miracle of grace, not us. In the early church, it was circumcision and eating food offered to idols; thirty years ago, it was the ordination of women; now it is human sexuality. We are called to be Church in the midst of the disagreement - in the midst of the muddle. Third, under the leadership of our Rector, the position of St. Paul's is clear. This is a community that welcomes all three groups. We welcome all voices. We dare not presume that there is a test of one's views to be a member or receive the Eucharist here at St. Paul's. We come with our views, differences, fears, and anxieties, and we receive the loving embrace of God. As Ephesians puts it, it is in Christ that we are built: it is into Christ that we live.

Lessons for the day:
John 6:1-21
Ephesians 3:14-21
Psalm 145:10-18
2 Kings 4:42-44

Chapter 3

Sermon on the theme of Citizenship

I love Britain. It is definitely part of me. However, on March 1, 2010 I became an American citizen. This was a sermon in which I reflected on this journey and shared with the congregation my perception of my new home.

'After this I looked and there was a great multitude that no one could count, from every nation, from all tribes and peoples and languages, standing before the throne and before the Lamb, robed in white, with palm branches in their hands.'

This remarkable vision of the life to come in the book of Revelation starts in an interesting place. Those participating in the worship of God are from 'every nation', 'from all tribes and peoples and languages'. We come to worship both now and in the life to come out of our particular story - out of our particular locale - out of our particular story. We come and gather out of our story around the throne to give worship to the God who gives us and enables us to be.

Coming out of a particular nation has been a preoccupying issue for my wife and me. After much thought and prayer, we have made the journey from subject of her Majesty the Queen to citizen of the United States. We took the vow, where we 'absolutely and entirely renounce and abjure all allegiance and fidelity to any foreign prince, potentate, state or sovereignty'.

Now naturally such a journey is not embarked on without much thought. We all still love the place in which we were born. A certain place, state, is the place where we grew up. And with it is a certain set of associations. So, for me the BBC is fabulous, Prime Ministers Question Time is great political drama; soccer is indeed a beautiful game and nothing can beat a warm summer evening at a 15th century pub eating 'steak and kidney pie'. And, of course, the place where family is will be forever special.

Yet we live in a world where people move from place to place. We form many 'homes'. One home is where we grow up; another home is where we are living now. And Lesley and I have decided to commit to the United States as our home. We have decided to commit to full participation in the civic life of this remarkable country.

Now naturally all nations (come to that all institutions) are mired in the reality of human sin. The British Empire was responsible for creation of nation states where the cartographers didn't exactly get it right; the British were behind the slave trade; and of course the United States participated in that trade and followed it up with segregation. These are deep evils that need to be recognized as such.

Recognizing all this, I confess to you all this morning that I am an Americaphile. I love all the bits you disapprove of - McDonalds' fries, Disney; I also admire the achievement of this country.

Courtesy of Susan Shillinglaw

And the achievement in a sentence is this: this is a country that witnessed to the possibility of being deeply committed to one's truth and at the same time equally committed to toleration. Where Europeans (much as I love them) solve the problem of religious coexistence by insisting that religion must be made to matter less (aggressive secularization), Americans are determined to witness to the possibility that one can be religiously committed and at the same insist that the right of another person to believe whatever is sacrosanct, even if that belief is misguided and will lead to hell. Truth meets toleration in a way that the world has found impossible for millennia. This place is for me a country that is called to witness to a possibility that for centuries we thought impossible: you can be deeply committed to the truth and allow others their error. It is possible to be in that place.

And so we return to the vision of heaven in the book of Revelations. As we gather this morning, we anticipate this vision. There are countless journeys in this room - from south to north, from rural to urban, from other nations to the United States. We are all on a journey. We bring our affection for a certain place. And we create new and different homes in different places. This is being human. And today, we gather with our particular stories to worship together. We don't deny our particular stories, instead we enjoy this moment of sharedness.

And Jesus in the Gospel reminds us of an important truth: whatever our journey, we are in his hands. We are sure of being safe. However, difficult the journey might be 'no one can snatch us out of his hand.' We are traveling and we are safe. How cool is that.

Lessons for the Day:
John 10:22-30
Acts 9:36-43
Psalm 23
Revelation 7:9-17

Chapter 4

After the Chapel Fire

Watching a chapel burn is horrendous. Watching the loss of holy space is jarring, difficult, and painful. This was a chapel that had stood for 129 years. This fire had occurred on Friday October 22 2010. This sermon was preached on the Monday October 25 2010 at Zabriskie Chapel of Immanuel Church on the Hill, which is across the road from the Seminary.

And so we gather for the first time as a community to celebrate the Eucharist after the fire.

Please notice the similarities: the prayer book is still there; people you like and love are still around you; the music is recognizable and familiar; Scripture is still speaking; later in this service we will be fed - the bread and wine will be transformed into the body and blood of our Lord. So much is the same.

Courtesy of Susan Shillinglaw

Yet, yet, yet. Bubbling underneath this service for each and every one of us is a deep sadness. To watch a worship space burn is difficult. It was not right. There is no way a 129 year old chapel should be taken in such a cruel and indecent way from us. It took just forty minutes to be unrecognizable. Windows that we learned to love are no longer part of our lives. A place full of associations, full of prayers, full of longings, full of struggle, full of fear, full of hope - a place that had absorbed all of this and more - has gone.

Anglicanism is a tactile tradition. Touch, space matters. We cross ourselves when we receive a blessing. We kneel or stand when we pray. We reverence the altar when we enter. We turn and face the Gospel when it is read. This is being Anglican; we are a tradition that believes that actions matters, that moving our body is part of the practice of worship, that space does indeed assume a holy significance.

Courtesy of Cayce Ramey

In that chapel of 129 years, there have been so many moments of holiness, it is impossible to count. The walls had heard it all. Countless seminarians have struggled, prayed, dreamed, and hoped on those pews. Thousands of seniors have delivered a sermon from that pulpit in front of their professors and peers. Morning Prayer had been said in that chapel - virtually every weekday morning since 1881. People have been baptized; people have been married; people have been buried; people have been ordained in the space.

Because God has done so much work in that space, it is a holy space. And as we watched the fire destroy the chapel, shatter the Ascension Window - it felt like an act of desecration.

We wanted to scream at God: this should not happen. It made us angry. It was disturbing.

It was painful.

Jesus doesn't explain why we live in a world where healing is necessary. Jesus doesn't explain why God allows human lives to be 'bound by Satan' for 18 years. There she was in excruciating pain. Instead Jesus steps in and does the work of healing. Our pain will be healed; we will be made whole. Indeed, the rich resources of Gospel will do much of that work today: we will be invited forward for the laying on of hands, we will be participating in the Eucharist, and we will be fed.

And so as we are healed, our pain is ameliorated, we are invited into the perspective of the Epistle. For the untransformed life, for the unredeemed life the picture is clear: we indulge in 'obscene, silly and vulgar talk', but for the redeemed life our author explains all this must be stopped, instead - and look how simple it is - 'let there be thanksgiving.'

It sounds silly, but it is so right. We don't indulge in unhelpful speculation. Or the misguided joke that hurts. Instead, we are thankful. And how can we be thankful when we are hurting? And so the Christian paradox of gratitude starts: we are thankful that no one was hurt; we are thankful for the uplifting worship of that week; we are thankful for the professionalism of the firefighters; we are thankful for the warmth and kindness of the rest of the Episcopal Church and beyond (Rabbi Moline has offered his worship space to us); we are thankful for this community that is determined to support and love each of us through it all.

And why is this 'gratitude' paradoxical? To the obvious question: why didn't God just stop the fire and save us all this 'after the event' gratitude? We are reminded that the Gospel is a paradox. In a moment our Celebrant will take us through 'The Great Thanksgiving'. And so we move through the drama in the Eucharistic prayer. We express our deep gratitude to God for the tragic loss of a human life at the age of 33. It sounds crazy. But it isn't. It is an act of trust that however strange things look at any particular moment, love will triumph. God will triumph. We will triumph. This is a triumphant act. And a worship space at this Seminary will emerge anew - soon and then in a more permanent way later.

This is the Gospel today. Jesus heals, even when we wish that we could live in a world where healing isn't necessary. This is the Gospel: seize it and trust it.

Lessons of the Day:
Ephesians 5:1-8
Luke 13:10-17
Psalm 37:27-33

Chapter 5

Out of the Ashes

The service started outside the Chapel Ruin. We took the opportunity to remember all those who had been commemorated on the plaques inside the chapel. We then processed into the Chapel for the Eucharistic service. This sermon wanted to link the themes of memory and tragedy together.

This past week, I marveled at the wisdom shared in a community email by our sister in Christ, Gina. From the vantage point of South Africa she wrote:

"I come from a culture where fire is part of the great circle of hope and life of the community. Before planting season (October-November), the fields are burnt. Some fires run off into nearby bushes, hills and mountains, reducing everything to heaps of ashes and the land lays bare. Soon the crack and the rumble of the summer thunders, lashed by startling lightening and heavy rains, become a source of hope and trembling.

Out of the ashes and trembling, new crops emerge, new blades of grass emerge, the field is again decorated with bright blooms; and fragrances of nature become pleasantly present. And hope for the community is restored. By December all the fields are green, the rolling hills and valleys are green. The birds and all wildlife return. Harvest season sets in and the feast of the first fruit is celebrated under the full moon with historic songs of triumph and thanksgiving…but it all begins with fire."

Today we give thanks "for all the saints." Gina remembers eloquently from her own culture that fire is "part of the great circle of hope and life." For the Church, the Saints of God are part of our "great circle of hope and life." This past Saturday, the Rt. Rev. Philip Alan Smith was commended to God and laid to rest in our cemetery. A distinguished professor and bishop, he was much loved throughout the Church. Many alumni made the journey back to campus to honor Bishop Smith. After the service and burial, memories filled the Deanery; the present was connected richly to Phil's life of service and 'hope for the community' was restored.

The act of holy remembrance is a Christian privilege, if not an obligation. The act of remembering makes us conscious of the past. It is so easy to turn the times of life—past, present and future—into idols. But it is also so easy to forget the past. The past must be cherished for it represents some faithful and hard work. It is the past that makes the present possible; it is the past that creates future possibilities. From time to time, it is important to revisit—to remember—the past.

We remember the past in order to be true and faithful in the present. We are grateful to the past for the possibilities that have been opened up to us. Yet, in the same way that we are not to idolize the present and future, we should not idolize the past. All time is judged by God, in whom all time is held in God's eternal life.

Bishop Smith was buried next to the grave of his college roommate and lifelong friend, the Rev. Charles Price. There is one word on Charles Price's tombstone: anamnesis. Price made that word central to his theology. He knew that it is in 'remembering' that we bring to God—the author of time—our own sense of the relationship of the past to the present and to the future. Price explains: 'To remember an experience in the presence of one who accepts means to live through it again, to appropriate it afresh in a new and creative (rather than destructive) way, hence to become more completely one's self. In this 'uncommon' understanding of remembering something of the living power of the word in its Biblical sense has been reborn.'

We are called when we remember the past not to be destroyed by it. This is the important part of the Gospel this day. The Chapel burned, the memories survived, and 'hope for the community' will be restored. We

Courtesy of Shireen Baker

do not languish in the past in a self-destructive way. Rather, we use the past to create resurrection possibilities now and in God's future.

Let our sacramental theology shape our response to this challenging moment in our present--as we give thanks for the Saints, that "great circle of hope and life" that surrounds us. Charlie Price saw anamnesis as a way of understanding or reconciling different understandings of the Holy Eucharist: "Recalling his death, resurrection and ascension, we offer you these gifts." In the act of recalling, of remembering, we participate in the moments of Jesus' life. Those saving moments are real to us. That is why we will always honor the past. It is our privilege and obligation as followers of Jesus Christ. We will not allow the past of last week to destroy this present moment, this All Saints Day. We will move beyond our life's grief and see bright possibilities for the future.

All Saints' Day is an act of holy remembrance. There is something lovely about All Saints. This festival gives us occasion to recognize all those who are not remembered, all those who do not have their own dedicated feast days. We remember the saints past and present who lived and live Luke's Beatitudes. These are the ones that the author of Ephesians remembers in prayer, these are the ones who names never made a plaque, yet made all the difference in ways unrecognized by the present. Our chapel shaped the past and the present not simply by those we remember but also by those whose names we can no longer call. However strange it might sound, on this day we remember with grateful hearts the unremembered.

Our service began as we gathered in the grove in front of the destroyed building which was our beloved Chapel. We remember those who are remembered on the walls and in the windows of that place. We honor, lift up, and name those who gave us that place which became holy by God's grace. We express our deep gratitude for all those who have labored in this vineyard before us, that 'great circle of hope and life,' to use Gina's words.

Today we give thanks that the Saints of God 'in glory shine.' We 'feebly struggle' now-- but out of the ashes of the present moment we pray for a future new and bright where 'hope is restored' and where God reigns for the ages of ages.

Lessons of the Day:
Luke 6: 20-31
Ephesians 1: 11-23
Psalm 149
Daniel 7:1-3, 15-18

Chapter 6

A Sermon on Faith and Doubt

St. Paul's Episcopal Church in Alexandria, Virginia is a thriving parish of over 3000 members. It has five services, which run from 5pm on Saturday night to 5pm on Sunday night. At a parish retreat, I discovered that many of the members of the parish struggle constantly with the plausibility of this or that aspect of the Christian story. This sermon was written in Advent to engage with those who cope with doubt. It was preached on December 12, 2010.

The text is Matthew 11:2 "Are you the one who is to come, or are we to wait for another?" asks John the Baptist to Jesus.

Exercising our reason can be tricky sometimes. Thinking through a problem can be hard work sometimes. There are so many factors to take into account. So, I am sure we are all familiar with the series of jokes intended to test our intelligence.

How do you get an Elephant into the Refrigerator?
Open the door and place the Elephant into the Refrigerator.

How do you get a Giraffe into the Refrigerator?
Open the door, take out the Elephant and then put the Giraffe into the Refrigerator.

The King of the Jungle calls a meeting of all the animals. Every single animal turns up save for one. Which one is it?
Well obviously the Giraffe – it is stuck in the Refrigerator.

You come to a crocodile infested river. There is no bridge, nor boat, and you must get across the river. How do you do it?

Easy you wade across. All the crocodiles are at the meeting called by the King of the Jungle.

Now normal acts of rationality are not quite as difficult as these. But often they are difficult. How do we know this or that is true? How do we know this or that is right?

In today's Gospel, this is the conundrum that John the Baptist faces. There he is paying the price for his ministry – sitting in a prison cell. And he wants to know whether Jesus is really the Messiah. So he sends his disciples to seek confirmation.

Let us pause right here. Asking the question is OK. Having doubts is OK. We are allowed to be 'not sure'. We are allowed to have questions. After all, it is a remarkable claim that Christians make. The creator of all that is discloses that reality in a child – as small as one of these children here being baptized. The Incarnation of God was a young Jewish boy living 2000 years. We are allowed to pause and say 'do we really believe this stuff?'

Now Jesus gives an interesting answer. He invites John the Baptist to revisit the expectations that the tradition has of the Messiah. The expectations we heard about in Isaiah. The Messiah will be an agent of healing, life, and love. So says Jesus – am I fulfilling these expectations? Am I an agent of healing, life, and love. If you can see that, then just trust it. Trust what you see and feel.

Faith is the act of thinking trust in what we see and feel of God's action around us. There are lots of reasons for belief in God – the fact that the universe is stable and explicable, our conviction that there is a moral order that we should observe, and supremely our sense that we are part of something bigger. But beyond these reasons, there are the experiences that point beyond – when we look at the miracle of a new born baby, we listen to *Panis Angelicus*, or see the sun coming up over Alexandria.

Courtesy of Susan Shillinglaw

Of course it is incredible to believe that God became a human baby at Christmas. If there are not moments when we doubt this remarkable claim, we are probably not understanding it. As it is often said 'the opposite of faith is not doubt, but certainty'. Too much certainty in religion can lead to hubris, intolerance, and cruelty. Doubt is part of faith – doubt is a recognition that with humility we believe in the amazing.

There is a reason why Rite 2 and the 1979 Prayer Book encourages us to say 'We believe' rather than 'I believe', when it comes to the creed. We are part of a community that helps us through the moments of doubt. We are letting the church help us with the hard work of believing. We are standing together and trusting that the church in its witness to the amazing has got it right.

Faith is the act of thinking trust in what we see and feel of God's action around us. From a dawn that inspires us to the laughter of friends – from the disclosure of an orderly universe in science to the amazing claim that God became vulnerable as a baby – faith is the act of thinking trust that all this discloses God to us. It was John Betjeman who put it so well, when he wrote:

> ....is it true? For if it is ....
>
> No love that in a family dwells,
>
> No caroling in frosty air,

Nor all the steeple-shaking bells

Can with this single Truth compare -

That God was man in Palestine

And lives today in Bread and Wine.

Lessons of the Day:
Isaiah 11:1-10
Romans 15:4-13
Matthew 3:1-12

Engagement

Chapter 7

Neither Conservative nor Liberal: A Theology of Christian Engagement with Non-Christian Traditions

Although it is an old joke, it is a revealing one. Two theologians are sitting next to each other. One is a liberal and the other an evangelical. The evangelical turns to the liberal and says, "I will call you a Christian provided you call me an intellectual'.

This is a revealing joke because it speaks to a particular perception. The liberal is the person who recognizes that faith needs to recognize its changed situation. Having read Kant and engaged with scientific thought, the liberal recognizes that there is a need to think differently about the faith. The liberal comes across as intelligent and engaged. Meanwhile the evangelical recognizes that faith is located in a tradition. Belonging to a tradition entitles a certain commitment to that tradition; given this the evangelical comes across as clearly committed to the Christian tradition.

Courtesy of Susan Shillinglaw

The purpose of this lecture is to challenge this popular perception of the difference between the liberal and evangelical (which in this paper, I am calling conservative, thereby including the conservative Roman Catholics). The argument involves four stages: first, there are certain core commitments that Christians wants to make, but those core commitments include the commitment to openness and liberality. Second, the tradition that Christians are called to affirm is demonstrably open and, crucially, willing to learn from non-Christian traditions. Therefore, third, the orthodox Christian should be open and constructively engaged with difference. And finally, Pope Benedict XVI is in danger of betraying a commitment to the openness of the Catholic tradition in his engagement with Islam.

Core Commitments

Christians follow Christ. Etymologically, this is what the word 'Christian' means. And, for Christians, the Christ is necessarily linked with two key doctrines – the Incarnation and the Trinity. These are our core commitments; for these doctrines provide the basis for our knowledge of God.

So let us unpack this a little. How do we know what God is like? The twin answers – natural and revealed theology – remain helpful. Following in the tradition of Aquinas, one might well feel able to deduce from the order in this world that it is more likely than not that there is a Creator. And if there is a Creator then this being must be some power (after all it is a big world to create) and some knowledge (after all you have to be pretty bright to create a world of this complexity). However, beyond these basics, natural theology cannot get us.[1]

So, as Karl Barth famously observed we need to recognize the importance of revealed theology.[2] Barth continues to be read because he gave us a straight choice, which makes considerable sense in our postmodern setting: either accept that God has revealed God's self in some place or make it all up – live like a guessing agnostic. And for Christians, the place of revelation - the Word of God - is a life – namely the life, death, and resurrection of Jesus.

---

[1] Aquinas took the view that Natural Theology could take us much further. However, this brief summary is where many contemporary philosophers of religion belong. For my own view, which is largely along these lines, see *Understanding Christian Doctrine*.

[2] Just to be clear, Karl Barth did not simply advocate revealed theology but insisted that 'revelation' was the only way a person could have knowledge of God. I would not go that far.

Barth is very helpful on the location of the Word. The Word of God is the place where you find a clear, definitive disclosure of God. Unlike for Muslims or Jews, the Word of God is not a text, but a life. Muslims misunderstand Christianity if it is assumed that the Bible is the equivalent to the Qur'an. This is wrong. It is the life, death, and resurrection of Jesus which is the Word and therefore the equivalent of the Qur'an. And in the same way as Muslims and Jews recognize that the Word of God must have always been (God has always uttered) and therefore believed in the pre-existence of the Qur'an and Torah, so Christians made a similar shift. The Word of God of John 1 is eternal.

Now unlike Judaism and Islam, the Christian tradition felt uncomfortable with two aspects of God sitting together in eternity past (namely, the Eternal Word and the Creator). It undermined our commitment to monotheism.[3] So the doctrine of the Trinity slowly emerged. The right way to understand God is as a dynamic entity that brings together the Creator with the Revealer and Redeemer. And to ensure that the actions of Creation and Redemption are not stuck in the past, so we talk about a third person who makes God present to us. We have three persons in one.

Our cornerstone commitments are bound to make the Christian tradition open and flexible. It is precisely because the Word of God, in Christianity, is not a text but a life that we find ourselves handling an adaptable Word. Of course, there is an important connection between the Word and the text of Scripture. For after all, it is the Bible that tells us about the Word, which is Jesus. And as Karl Barth put it the Bible becomes the Word as it witnesses to the Word which is Jesus.[4] Nevertheless the primary Word is the Eternal Word which completely interpenetrates the life of Jesus of Nazareth.

---

[3] I am very grateful for the work of Thomas Michel on the Trinity.
[4] For Karl Barth's view of Scripture see Church Dogmatics I/2, p. 530. See also the very helpful lecture in this same series by Professor Douglas John Hall, called 'Who can say it as it is. Karl Barth on the Bible'http://www.christchair.ucalgary.ca/cevents.html (accessed January 26, 2007).

As Christians, we are in the business of reading a life – a life, which was very enigmatic. Our definitive disclosure of what God is like is a poor young man from Nazareth, who took enormous risks as he reached out to include the marginalized – especially women, the poor, and the reviled. He found himself a victim of power – finally dying as a common criminal at the hands of the occupying power. Yet remarkably, the movement he birthed believed that death was not able to hold him. Reports of his resurrection started to circulate and so the church was born.

So what do we know about God? We know that God is on the side of those who are least fortunate. We know that the love of God is willing to go to any length for the sake of humanity. We know that in our moments of despair, God promises to create hope. We know that we should treat this life as authoritative. We should imitate the 'words and deeds' of Jesus of Nazareth.

Courtesy of Susan Shillinglaw

Now, our obligation as Christians is to recognize the authority of this life in guiding our witness today. This obligation extends to our interpretation of the rest of the Bible. If the Bible is interpreted in such a way to contract what we 'read' from the life, death, and resurrection of the Eternal Word, then we have an obligation to revisit the text of the Bible. Although slavery is instituted in Leviticus and condoned in 1 Timothy, the legitimacy of slavery is clearly incompatible with the disclosure of God in the life, death, and resurrection of Jesus.

Unlike reading the Qur'an, it is difficult to read a life. So, Christians are right from the outset bound to have to live with a pluralism of positions. Although the slave-traders are outside the zone of acceptable pluralism, there are a multitude of positions with which the life of Jesus might be compatible. The areas of debate include the following: gratuitous war is clearly unacceptable, but the use of force to create a just peace might be acceptable; exploitative capitalism is clearly wrong, but the use of the profit motive to create an effective system of resource allocation might be acceptable; and reading a life does have a major advantage over a text. It permits significant flexibility over time. We are imitating the 'words and deeds' of Jesus. This exercise starts in the New Testament and we can see how the Church struggles to arrive at the appropriate inclusive position over the Gentiles and the Jewish Law. And so it continues with Augustine and Aquinas.

The movement for Christian thought is to constantly move, to and fro, from the life, death, and resurrection of Jesus of Nazareth (as it flows through the sacraments and life of the Church) to the particularities of each situation. With the Spirit of God constantly making the Eternal Word present to each situation, we can and should allow our faith to engage with each situation making use of all the resources available to us. The resources flow from our conviction of the three-fold nature of God: a creator who creates every single life and loves each particular life and seeks to disclose truth to those lives; a revealer and redeemer who discloses the nature of God (thereby providing a definitive norm) and also redeems all people; and a Spirit who is constantly making God present and allowing us to see God in new and different ways.

These core convictions are responsible for a theology which is constantly engaging and changing. It might be ironic: but to be completely orthodox, one should be liberal.

The Christian Tradition

The epitome of an orthodox theology is Augustine of Hippo. If I can show that Augustine is really a liberal, then my case will be complete. Naturally, such an argument will upset both the conservatives and the liberals. The conservatives do feel Augustine is a model theologian who is completely faithful to the Christian witness and would be appalled to learn that Augustine is really a liberal. The liberals take pride in rejecting the Christian tradition. For Bishop John Shelby Spong, for example, the tradition is in deep error: and a modern form of Christianity needs to repudiate those errors. So let us look more closely at this hugely significant figure.[5]

Let us concede that there aspects of Augustine which are problematic. The exercise of finding shocking passages in Augustine is a game that many like to play. For example, there is his doctrine of massa peccatrix as stated in *De Natura et Gratia* where Augustine writes:

> This grace of Christ, then, without which neither children nor adults can be saved, is given gratuitously and not for our merits, and for this reason it is called "grace.""[They are] justified," says the Apostle, "freely by his blood." Consequently, those who are not liberated through grace, either because they have not yet been able to hear, or because they have not wished to obey, or also because, when on account of their age they were not capable of hearing, they did not receive the bath of regeneration, which they could have received and by means of which they would have been saved, are justly condemned. For they are not without sin, either that which they contracted originally or that which they added through their own misconduct. "For all have sinned," either in Adam or in themselves, "and are deprived of the glory of God." Consequently, the whole human mass ought to be punished, and if the deserved punishment of damnation were rendered to all, beyond all doubt it would be justly rendered. This is why those who are liberated from it by grace are not called vessels of their own merits but "vessels of mercy."[6]

Most Christians are unhappy with Augustine's views on predestination, which is linked with his conviction that only a minuscule number of people will be saved; and for his view that unbaptized infants are damned to hell, it is not surprising that limbo was invented by the

---

[5] This section on Augustine is an edited (and reduced) version of the material found in my Theology of Engagement Chapter 2.
[6] Augustine, *De Natura et Gratia* IV 4 -V 5.

medieval church. The package of original sin and eternal damnation is held to be responsible for a multitude of difficulties. Adherents in other faith traditions find his exclusivism problematic. Feminist theologians blame Augustine for a dualism (inherited from his neo-Platonism) that celebrates spirit and denigrates the body.[7] This, they argue, has directly underpinned patriarchy. The male was considered more spiritual and the female was less spiritual because of a link with sex and nature. The evidence for this analysis is built on Augustine's intricate analysis of the possibility of sexual intercourse found in his *City of God*: there, you will recall, Augustine arrives at the extraordinary view that prior to the Fall, passionless sex that leaves women in a virginal state would have been possible.

So to suggest that Augustine can also be a liberal hero seems manifestly problematic.

Surely he is the great villain? My argument will be that methodologically Augustine is a liberal and therefore sympathetic to a theology of engagement. The argument is simple: Augustine's methodology involves three central components. First, reason clearly has a central role. Second, he draws heavily on non-Christian sources. Third, the experience of his life transformed by Christ and therefore is the centrality of 'experience.' I shall show that in these three elements we have a surprisingly modern methodology operating: reason, the use of non-Christian wisdom, and experience. It is his willingness to learn from a range of sources that is Augustine's great strength. It is also this willingness that must make it both legitimate (in that it is true to Augustine's own method) and necessary to develop the tradition.

---

[7] See Anne Primavesi, *From Apocalypse to Genesis: ecology, feminism and Christianity* (Minneapolis: Fortress Press 1991). It is a moot point the extent to which these criticisms are justified. A. Hilary Armstrong makes a strong case that both Christians and Platonists have a much more positive view of the body and the material universe than opponents give them credit for: he writes, 'Augustine in particular is often more balanced and positive – and not, as sometimes seems to be assumed, more unbalanced and negative – in his attitude to the body, sex and marriage than most of his Christian contemporaries.' (See A. Hilary Armstrong, *St. Augustine and Christian Platonism* (Villanova: Villanova University Press 1976) p.11.

Saint Augustine of Hippo

At the most basic level: if we start by considering a commitment to 'reason' as involving the recognition of the importance of our human rational capacity and therefore the importance of reason and good logical arguments, then no one can doubt Augustine's commitment to reason. Good arguments pervade his work: intellectual puzzles are stated and grappled with. There are numerous illustrations of this: for example, his reflections on the nature of time at the end of the *Confessions* or the problem of human knowledge and divine foreknowledge discussed in the *City of God*.[8]

His commitment to reason also arises out of his anthropology. So in *De Animae Quantitate* (On the greatness of the soul), Augustine writes, 'If you wish a definition of what the soul is, I have a ready answer. It seems to be a certain kind of substance, sharing in reason, fitted to rule the body.'[9] Later in *De trinitate*, Augustine writes:

> Desiring to train the Reader in the things that were made, in order that he might know Him by whom they were made, we have now at last arrived at His image which is man, in that whereby He is superior to other animals, namely, in reason and understanding, and whatever else can be said of the rational or intellectual soul that pertains to that thing which is called the mind or animus.[10]

---

[8] See *The Confessions* Book 11 and The City of God Book 5 Chapter 9.
[9] *De Animae Quantitate* (On the greatness of the soul) chapter 13. Unless otherwise stated all translations are taken from The Fathers of the Church.
[10] *De trinitate* Book 15 Chapter 1.

The mind then, for Augustine, is the highest point of the soul. So it is not surprising that Augustine has a high regard for the rational capacity of the mind. Etienne Gilson brings out the significance of this for Augustine's view of the relationship between faith and reason when he points out that for Augustine 'the very possibility of faith depends on reason. Of all the beings God created on earth, only man is capable of belief, because he alone is endowed with reason. Man exists, as do wood and stones; he lives, as the plants do; he moves and feels, as do animals; but in addition, he thinks. Moreover the mind, whereby man knows what is intelligible, is in his case the mark man left of His handiwork: it is in the mind that he is made in God's image. . . .In short, man is the image of God inasmuch as he is a mind which, by exercising its reason, acquires more and more understanding and grows progressively richer therein.'[11]

Additional evidence that reason and good arguments mattered to Augustine is demonstrated in his capacity to revisit older arguments and to correct them. The *Retractationes* is a remarkable phenomenon that reflects well on his commitment to intellectual integrity. The opening of the *Retractationes* reflects both this commitment and a delightful self-deprecating irony. He writes:

> For a long time I have been thinking about and planning to do something which I, with God's assistance, am now undertaking because I do not think it should be postponed: with a kind of judicial severity, I am reviewing my works -- books, letters, and sermons -- and, as it were, with the pen of a censor, I am indicating what dissatisfies me. For, truly, only an ignorant man will have the hardihood to criticize me for criticizing my own errors. But if he maintains that I should not have said those things which, indeed, dissatisfied me later, he speaks the truth and concurs with me. In fact, he and I are critics of the same

---

[11] Etienne Gilson, *The Christian Philosophy of St. Augustine* (New York: Random House 1960) p.29.

thing, for I should not have criticized such things if it had been right to say them.[12]

It might be objected that too much is being made of the obvious intellectual depth of Augustine - this is after all why he is so widely read and why he was so influential. The point being stressed however is the important but often overlooked fact that Augustine was rigorously self-critical and committed to formulating an account of faith that was both coherent and justified in terms of good arguments.

The second area is his use of non-Christian traditions to shape this theology. Once again, in much the same way that 'reason', interpreted as a commitment to good argument, is universally affirmed as true of Augustine's work so everyone agrees that Augustine was certainly shaped by his reading of neo-Platonism (the Platonism of Platonius and beyond). But as with the debate about the extent of reason's involvement with authority, so there is a comparable debate about neo-Platonism.

At one extreme we have Adolf von Harnack who in 1888 argued that at the conversion, Augustine was no more than a Platonist influenced by Christianity rather than the other way round. At the other extreme we have G. Quispel who argued that there is no important doctrine in Augustine that is not grounded in the Bible.[13] The truth, like so many of these debates, is firmly in between.

There are two areas that require exploration. First is the influence of neo-Platonism on his conversion; and second is Augustine's explicit sympathies for neo-Platonism and his interpretation of their insights. It will be shown that Augustine affirms truth where ever it is found and allows non-Christian insights to shape his Christianity.

We start then with the influence of neo-Platonism on his conversion. The primary source for this is the *Confessions*. Perhaps a comment is

---

[12] *Retractionarie* Prologue.
[13] See G. Quispel, *Eranos-Jahrbuch* (1951) pp.115-40 as cited in John J. O'Meara, *Understanding Augustine* (Dublin: Four Courts Press 1997) p.92.

necessary on the attention I propose to give the *Confessions*. There are difficulties here: first it is not a traditional autobiography; it is more a chronicle of the journey of the heart. The traditional background to a biography is entirely neglected. So while we are fascinated by his concubine and find ourselves indignant about his decision to send her back to Africa because his career needs a socially advantageous marriage, this does not concern Augustine. What troubles us is not what troubles Augustine. Given the conventions of his age, this was not an issue. Second, some have questioned the historicity of the Confessions. For example, in the Confessions Augustine decides to leave his teaching post for religious reasons, elsewhere he suggests that he leaves on the grounds of ill-health. It is not my purpose to defend the Confessions, although I do take the view that most of the apparent discrepancies identified are more imagined than proven.[14] Anyway my interest in Augustine is methodological, and given this the precise historicity is unimportant.

It is clear that Augustine's underlying principle is that all 'truth belongs to God.' So, a love of wisdom wherever it is found drives Augustine on. He writes,

> In Greek the word 'philosophy' means 'love of wisdom', and it was with this love that the Hortensius inflamed me. There are people for whom philosophy is a means of misleading others, for they misuse its great name, its attractions, and its integrity to give colour and gloss to their own errors. Most of these so-called philosophers who lived in Cicero's time and before are noted in the book. . . (T)he only thing that pleased me in Cicero's book was his advice not simply to admire one or another of the schools of philosophy, but to love wisdom itself, whatever it

---

[14] Alfred Matthews sets out the debate with some care. His response to the difficulties, I largely find persausive. See Alfred Warren Matthews, *The Development of St. Augustine from Neoplatonism to Christianity 386-391AD* (Washington: University Press of America 1980) pp7-10.

might be, and to search for it, pursue it, hold it, and embrace it firmly.[15]

Cicero's Hortensius is Augustine's way into philosophy. From it, Augustine learns the importance of seeking wisdom. As Augustine became disillusioned with Manichaeism, so he discovered neo-Platonism (probably the writings of Plotinus). He finds in these writings good arguments for the existence of God and his eternal word. Augustine explains:

> So you [i.e. God] made use of a man, one who was bloated with the most outrageous pride, to procure me some of the books of the Platonists, translated from the Greek into Latin. In them I read - not, of course, word for word, though the sense was the same and it was supported by all kinds of different arguments – that at the beginning of time the Word already was; and God had the Word abiding with him, and the Word was God. . . .In the same books I also read of the Word, God, that his birth came not from human stock, not from nature's will or man's, but from God. But I did not read in them that the Word was made flesh and came to dwell among us.[16]

Augustine's readings in Neoplatonism persuade him of God and the eternal word, although there is nothing about the Incarnation. He treats the illumination that these books provide him about God as intended by God. Although Cicero and Platonius are non-Christians, he has no difficulty in acknowledging the truth about God he finds within their writing.

The second area we need to explore is his explicit treatment of Neo-Platonism in some of his writings. Although in the Retractions he does express disquiet about the extent of his praise and admiration, the praise and admiration is still there and presumably reflects his view at the

---

[15] St. Augustine, *Confessions* trans. by R. S. Pine-Coffin (Harmondsworth: Penguin 1961) p.59.
[16] Ibid. p.144-5. (Book 7:9).

time. The discussions of Neo-Platonism are extensive that selection is a major difficulty. Both in terms of content and method, the Neo-Platonism is important. On the content front, we find in *Civitas Dei* that Augustine explicitly lists the connections between neoplatonism and Christianity. John O'Meara, helpful summarizes thus, 'They [i.e. the neoplatonists] taught the existence of an incorporeal Creator, of Providence, the immortality of the soul, the honor of virtue, patriotism, true friendship, and good morals. Final happiness, moreover, they held to be attainable through participation of the soul in the Creator's unchangeable and incorporeal light.'[17] On the method front, Etienne Gilson insists that Augustine's debt to Plotinus is considerable. He writes, 'To Plotinus he is indebted for almost all the matter and for the whole technique of his philosophy. He is indebted to the Bible for the basic Christian notions which compelled him to make the inner transformation he performed on the Plotinian theses he borrowed and to construct in this way a new doctrine which represents one of the first, and one of the most original contributions Christianity has made to enrich the history of philosophy.'[18] Interestingly given the next chapter, Gilson goes on to draw an explicit parallel between Augustine and Aquinas, he writes, '[A]ll we can say is that he did for Plotinus what St. Thomas Aquinas was later to do for Aristotle, i.e. to make, in the light of faith, a rational revision of a great philosophical interpretation of the universe.'[19]

Indeed such was his regard for the Neo-Platonist, that he makes two striking claims:

> 1. If Plato was alive today, then he would be a Christian.
> 2. Plato has so much insight that it seems plausible to believe that he must of learned from Jeremiah the great Jewish prophet.

For the first this can be seen in *On True Religion*. Augustine writes,

---

[17] John J. O'Meara, *Understanding Augustine* (Dublin: Four Courts Press 1997) p.84-5.
[18] Etienne Gilson, *The Christian Philosophy of St. Augustine* (New York: Random House 1960) p.234.
[19] Ibid. p.234.

Suppose Plato were alive and would not spurn a question I would put to him; or rather suppose one of his own disciples, who lived at the same time as he did, had addressed him thus: "You have persuaded me that truth is seen not with the bodily eyes but by the pure mind, and that any soul that cleaves to truth is thereby made happy and perfect. . . .Therefore the mind has to be healed so that it may behold the immutable form of things which remains ever the same, preserving its beauty unchanged and unchangeable, knowing no spatial distance or temporal variation, abiding absolutely one and the same. . . To the rational and intellectual soul is given to enjoy the contemplation of eternity, and by that contemplation it is armed and equipped so that it may obtain eternal life. . . . You, my master, have persuaded me to believe these things. Now, if some great and divine man should arise to persuade the peoples that such things were to be at least believed if they could not grasp them with mind, or that those who could grasp them should not allow themselves to be implicated in the depraved opinions of the multitude or to be overborne by vulgar errors, would you not judge that such a man is worthy of divine honors?" I believe Plato's answer would be: "That could not be done by man, unless the very virtue and wisdom of God delivered him from natural environment, illumined him from his cradle not by human teaching but by personal illumination, honored him with such grace, strengthened him with such firmness and exalted him with such majesty, that he should be able to despise all that wicked men desire, to suffer all that they dread, to do all that they marvel at, and so with the greatest love and authority to convert the human race to so sound a faith." . . . Now this very thing has come to pass.[20]

The argument here is interesting and subtle. Platonism discovered the problem facing human existence: knowledge of the good, the true, and

---

[20] *De vera religione* iii, 3 - 4. Translation taken from St. Augustine, On True Religion, Introduction by L. O. Mink, translated J.H.S. Burleigh, (South Bend, Indiana: Regnery/Gateway 1953).

the beautiful depends on transcending our human propensity to lust and preoccupation with matter. However, if Plato was asked, 'don't we need a person who can demonstrate how this is possible?' Plato would reply 'yes, but it would be very difficult.' And this, argues Augustine, is precisely what has come to pass.

Saint Augustine by Phillipe de Champaigne

The third element is 'experience'. He admits that he is driven to the doctrine of the Incarnation because he needs the strength to enjoy God. He writes, 'I began to search for a means of gaining the strength I needed to enjoy you, but I could not find this means until I embraced the mediator between God and men, Jesus Christ, who is a man, like them, and also rules as God over all things, blessed forever.'[21] John Rist captures Augustine's meaning extremely well when he writes, 'Neoplatonism is incomplete; its underlying weakness is that it is theoretical, without the power to instigate right action.'[22]

Augustine finds the 'power' at the end of book eight of *The Confessions*. He is in a Milanese garden in August 386, tormented by sinfulness and asking God to explain why it was all so difficult. Then he writes:

> I was asking myself these questions, weeping all the while with most bitter sorrow in my heart, when all at once I heard the sing-

---

[21] *Civitas Dei* Ibid. p.153. (Book 7:18)
[22] John Rist, *Augustine* (Cambridge: Cambridge University Press 1994) p.3.

song voice of a child in a nearby house. Whether it was the voice of a boy or a girl I cannot say, but again and again it repeated the refrain 'Take it and read, take it and read'. At this I looked up, thinking hard whether there was any kind of game in which children used to chant words like these, but I could not remember ever hearing them before. I stemmed my flood of tears and stood up, telling myself that this could only be a divine command to open my book of Scripture and read the first passage on which my eyes should fall. . . . So I hurried back to the place where Alypius was sitting, for when I stood up to move away I had put down the book containing Paul's Epistles. I seized it and opened it, and in silence I read the first passage on which my eyes fell: Not in revelling and drunkenness, not in lust and wantonness, not in quarrels and rivalries. Rather, arm yourselves with the Lord Jesus Christ; spend no more thought on nature and nature's appetites. I had no wish to read more and no need to do so. For in an instant, as I came to the end of the sentence, it was as though the light of confidence flooded into my heart and all the darkness of doubt was dispelled.[23]

This is an old-fashioned religious experience. As many others have, before and since, Augustine tormented by his moral failures, finds in Jesus a confidence that he can triumph over sin.

Once again the term 'experience' has a potentially anachronistic association. It is not the case that Augustine is the same as Schleiermacher. Instead, it is more accurate to say that Augustine would not want to separate his experience from his philosophy. Armstong is helpful here when he insists that for Augustine and his contemporaries there is no distinction between philosophy and theology: 'It was an activity embracing the whole of human life, an attempt not merely to direct but to bring man to his goal through an understanding of the whole of reality. . . . If this is what philosophy meant, it is easy to see

---

[23] St. Augustine, *Confessions* trans. by R. S. Pine-Coffin (Harmondsworth: Penguin 1961) (Book 8. Part 12) p.177-8.

that for Christians the only true philosophy could be nothing else but a lived and living theology, a reflection on the mysteries of faith, using all the resources of a Greek-trained intelligence, which determined the Christian way of life.'[24]

Although Augustine would not appreciate my attempt to disentangle three sources of his theology, I want to suggest that the case can be made that Augustine arrives at faith using these three sources: reason, non-Christian sources of wisdom, and experience. So, now bringing Augustine together with the cornerstone section, we now have the following. Augustine is transformed by a sense of Jesus. As he seeks to live life true to that core commitment, he continues to use his reason, welcome and embrace movement in his thought, and crucially learn from non-Christian traditions. He uses platonic terminology in his understanding of the faith. For Augustine, 'reading the life of Jesus' was difficult. Methodologically, he is clearly liberal. And even if we would now reject some of his conclusions as incompatible with the core disclosure of God in Jesus of Nazareth, we can still relate to his struggle to discern the truth and interpret the pressures on his situation in the light of his understanding of what God reveals in Christ.

Courtesy of Susan Shillinglaw

What is true of Augustine is also true of other great theologians. Aquinas, for example, is trained as an Augustinian Platonist and then engages with the philosopher Aristotle. In addition, he thinks through his faith in conversation with Jewish and Islamic thinkers. However, for

---

[24] A. Hilary Armstrong, 'Reason and Faith in the First Millenium A.D.' in A. Hilary Armstong, Plotinian and Christian Studies (London: Variorum Reprints 1979) p.108.

the purposes of time, I am confining myself to one illustration. Suffice it to say, Christians who seek to be true to the Tradition should be open to non-Christian influences and insights.

Orthodox Christians are Liberal

So we arrive at the slogan of this lecture. Orthodox Christians should be liberal. Grounded in the core convictions of our faith, we are called to apply our reason and search for a recognition of what the Spirit of God is saying through the encounter with difference. In one sense, this is the classic Roman Catholic position. For this position shares with Rome an appropriate emphasis upon both tradition and Scripture. And it understands Christian entirely through the prism of Jesus. In addition, it builds on a Catholic anthropology. Such an anthropology takes issue both with the 19th century optimistic view of humanity (we are all good really) and with the pessimistic anthropology of the Reformed tradition (we are all completely depraved). Instead we are both/and. We are made in the image of God (and therefore have the capacity for some limited right reasoning about the world and morality) and simultaneously we are fallen (and therefore have constant propensities towards egoism and selfishness). Such an anthropology would strongly suggest that all religions contain both insight and error – Christianity included. Given this, we have an obligation to learn of God from the encounter with the other.

A constructive, engaged theology which is grounded in our core convictions disclosed in the life, death, and resurrection of Jesus should be the Christian attitude to other faith traditions. The act of dialogue where you learn of God those truths that are not contained in our tradition, but are nevertheless compatible with the core convictions is an act of Christian faithfulness. Countless Christians have discovered this. Pioneers who lived this spirit settled in India, learnt from Sufis, and have been shaped by Rabbis. Such pioneers are models that we should seek to emulate.

However, the new Pope has started his pontiff with an attack on Islam. So this paper will conclude with a brief analysis and description of that attack.

Pope Benedict XVI

Let it be acknowledged right at the outset that Pope Benedict XVI is an exceptionally able theologian: he is well read and creative in the way in which he engages with the tradition. He is starting his Papacy with a certain set of concerns which are interesting and significant. He is getting much that is right. However, it is my view that the Regensburg speech was not simply unhelpful and impolitic, but also a fundamental betrayal of the tradition he leads. This is a serious allegation: so let us examine briefly the concerns that are preoccupying this Pope and how the Regensburg speech fits into those concerns.

His first major concern is European Christianity. Taking the name Benedict was deliberate. Benedict, as Alasdair MacIntyre famously reminded us in After Virtue, created the forms of monastic life which kept the tradition of the virtues alive during the first dark ages. Pope Benedict shares with MacIntyre a concern about the spirit and shape of modernity as it has formed and developed in Europe: Europe is in the midst of a new dark ages. And he sees the task of his Papacy is to call Europe back to its religious roots. A civilized culture needs to be grounded in the Christian tradition.

His second major concern is Islam. And it is here that I wish to focus.

His lecture in Germany at the University of Regensburg on 12 September 2006 provoked considerable controversy. So, let us start by looking at that lecture with some care. The argument of the lecture can be examined in five stages.

First, he starts by exploring the Christian Muslim dialogue of the late 14th century between the 'Byzantine emperor Manuel II Paleologus and an educated Persian.'[25] The Pope endorses the view that the verses in the Qur'an friendly to religious diversity (e.g. Sura 2:256 'there is no compulsion in religion') were written in Mecca and were superseded by the verses in Medina which justify holy war. The Pope does imply that there is a tension in the Qur'an between a pro-pluralism strand (formulated when the Prophet is weak) and an intolerant strand (formulated when the Prophet had power).

Second, after quoting the Emperor's view of the Muhammad's 'evil and inhuman' contribution to the history of ideas, the Pope arrives at the key thought of his lecture, namely that the use of violence to further faith is unreasonable.

Third, the Pope draws a contrast between the development of Christianity, which is a mixture of Hebrew and Greek thought, and the emergence of Islam. For Christians, the Gospel of John is 'the final word on the biblical concept of God.' In John 1, the logos, explains the Pope, means 'both reason and word – a reason which is creative and capable of self-communication, precisely as reason.' For the Pope, God's providence ensured the meeting of the Biblical drama and Hellenistic thought: and the result is that Christianity recognizes that 'reason' is a control on faith. For Christians, we can be confident that God will not command the 'irrational'.

By implication, the Pope suggests that Islam is not so fortunate. The Pope explains, 'But for Muslim teaching, God is absolutely transcendent. His will not bound up with any of our categories, even that of rationality.' Indeed he cites Ibn Hazn (the Spanish Muslim thinker of the 11th century) as an example of a thinker who advocated 'the image of a capricious God, who is not even bound to truth and goodness.'

Fourth, the problem of Islam is also the problem of the Modern West. At this point, he suggests there are three factors that are underpinning

---

[25] All quotations from the lecture are taken from the version provided by the Vatican and available on the BBC website.

modernity which are leading to a 'dehellenization' (i.e. the erosion of the Greek commitment to rationality). The first was the Reformation; the second was the liberal theology of the nineteenth and twentieth century. And the third is 'cultural pluralism' or to put it more accurately the quest to create a non-Hellenistic form of Christianity which is found behind the New Testament (I suspect the Pope is thinking here of the work of the Protestant theologian John Hick).

Fifth, he concludes the lecture for Europe as a whole to retain and recover the Catholic (presumably because the Reformation undermined it) commitment to faith and rationality. It is not a call to go back: instead 'the positive aspects of modernity are to be acknowledged unreservedly'. But it is a call for 'faith and reason to come together in a new way' – one in which 'we overcome the self-imposed limitations of reason to the empirically verifiable'.

This in five stages is the Pope's lecture. Reactions to the lecture have ranged widely. We had Muslim rage in parts of the Islamic world, where the most dramatic quotations were taken out of context and used to create riots. Ratzinger the academic was in conflict with Benedict XVI the Pope. Where the Cardinal could have delivered this lecture with virtually no interest being provoked, the Pope is the major leader of Christendom. Muslims are feeling battered: they have had to cope with colonialism, corrupt regimes supported by the West, constant denigration of their faith by a richer and more affluent western academy, and of course the running sore of the Palestinian people and the invasion of Iraq. For the leader of the world's Catholics to decide to quote – in passing and for illustrative purposes only – a medieval attack on Islam was bad politics.

For the contrasting reaction, we have been those who have talked about this lecture as the 'the Regensburg Moment'. Richard John Neuhaus, the Roman Catholic theocon (to coin Damon Linker's phrase[26]), writes:

---

[26] See Damon Linker, *Theocons*.

> Benedict has expressed regret about the violent Muslim reaction to what he said; he has continued to meet with Muslim leaders; he has reaffirmed the Church's continuing dialogue with Islam – but there is no chance whatsoever that he will retract or retreat from the argument he has made.[27]

For Neuhaus, this was not a speech written by a Vatican official who did not appreciate the significance of what was being said. This was entirely deliberate. This is Benedict's view. Neuhaus even feels that the quotation of the medieval emperor was appropriate: Neuhaus writes, 'But the citation was also a way of reminding everyone that this conflict with Islam bent upon conversion by the sword is very long-standing'.[28] For Neuhaus, the Pope is an uncomplicated ally. The Pope sees theglobal threat posed by the jihadists who want to 'destroy the West … and force the world's submission to Islam.'[29]

Now I suspect that Neuhaus is right in his interpretation of the Pope's intentions. And if so, then I wish to identify with those many Roman Catholics who are awkward that this is the Pope's position. Granted, there is much that is interesting about the Pope's position. He is right about the need for the West to hold 'faith' and 'reason' together. He is also right to insist that Christian minorities should be treated as well as Muslim minorities are in the West. But there are major difficulties in his position: one at the level of detail and the other, more importantly, at the level of spirit.

At the level of detail, there are assumptions made in this lecture which are mistaken. There is much greater continuity between the earlier suras in Mecca and the later suras in Medina. The Constitution of Medina, for example, did protect the entitlement of the people of the book to worship. It is not true to say that Islam was unaffected by the Greek

---

[27] Richard John Neuhaus, 'The Regensburg Moment' in First Things, 167 (November 2006):59.
[28] Richard John Neuhaus, 'On the Square: Observations and Contentions' Septermber 18 2006 at www.firstthings.com (accessed 21 November 2006).
[29] Ibid.

commitment to rationality; after all, it was Islamic culture that kept Aristotle's writings alive. And as in Christianity, there is the spectrum of positions. And in our comparative histories, the Christian does have to face the fact that in Syria and Egypt significant Christian communities survived Islamic rule, but no significant Muslim communities survived Christian rule (see, for example, Spain). And in terms of the contemporary threat from Muslims, we need to recognize that there is, for example, a large and growing non-violent dialogical form of Turkish Islam, namely the Nur movement. The failure to do so is to leave the world with a distorted view of the relations between traditions.

At the level of spirit, we see a Pope who is, I suggest, not being true to the dynamics of the Roman Catholic tradition. It is incompatible with Catholic anthropology to demonize a people. It is incompatible with the tradition's obligation to listen to the Spirit of God to generalize about the failure of Islam to reconcile faith with reason. Perhaps most seriously, it is incompatible with what we know of God in Christ to fail to see the 'fruits of the Spirit' in countless Muslim lives.

In one sense, this is unfair to Pope Benedict. His subsequent trip to Turkey was adept and skillful in building bridges with the Catholic Church and Turkish Islam. His 2005 address on World Youth Day, he stressed the need for dialogue with Muslims and that both Muslims and Christians 'agree on the fact that terrorism of any kind is a perverse and cruel choice which shows contempt for the sacred right to life and undermines the very foundations of all civil coexistence.'[30] This sort of talk is much more compatible with the Catholic tradition he is called to represent.

It might be odd for an Episcopalian to accuse an exceptionally erudite Pope that he is failing to represent the tradition which he leads. However, the Christian-Muslim dialogue is central at this moment. And

---

[30] Pope Benedict, World Youth Day, Cologne.

I offer these reflections in the hope that the Christian communities can engage appropriately with Islam in all its diversity.

Conclusion

We live in an odd world. Conservatives imagine they are upholding the tradition by asking us to accept the unchanged message of our past. Liberals imagine they are challenging the tradition by asking us to reject the injustice, patriarchy, and racism of our past. Conservatives and liberals agree that the past is monolithic: one side insisting we need to still affirm it, the other insisting we need to reject it.

Courtesy of Susan Shillinglaw

The truth is that we should be continuing to affirm the method of our tradition – a tradition that constantly engages afresh as our core convictions about the God disclosed in Christ encounters our historic moment. Our historic moment makes the encounter with Islam central.

And gently I have attempted to show that the Pope Regensburg speech was not in the spirit of the tradition he represents.

It is always tempting to over-simplify the other. But oversimplification is one thing we cannot afford. Faithfulness to our tradition involves a recognition of the complexity of the difference we constantly encounter.

The Lebel Lectures on Christian Ethics given at University of Calgary, Canada.

Chapter 8

Open Orthodoxy and Same-Sex Marriage: Where Should Christians Stand?

Freud and St. Augustine of Hippo have lots in common. They both recognize the significance of the sexual realm in human life. Freud is famous for the way in which he found overwhelming 'evidence about the significant part that sexual factors play in the neuroses.'[1] Augustine in *The Confessions* talks of 'sensual folly assumed domination over me, and I gave myself totally to it in acts allowed by shameful but under your laws illicit.'[2] He admits he enjoyed satisfying his lust: he writes, 'when I prayed you for chastity and said: "Grant me chastity and continence, but not yet." I was afraid you might hear my prayer quickly, and that you might too rapidly heal me of the disease of lust which I preferred to satisfy rather than suppress.'[3] For Augustine, the sexual is so central to human identity that disordered desires in this realm permeates every other aspect of our lives. And in a strange way, Freud would concur. For Freud, the inappropriate recognition of our sexual desires will result in physical and mental illness. Although the political expression of their thought would differ, they share the view that sexuality is unavoidably significant.

The struggle of Europe and North America to form a view about the range of lifestyle options, which are entitled to public recognition, witnesses to the significance of sex in our culture. In a world where global warming threatens to overwhelm us and half the world's

---

[1] Ernest Jones, *The Life and Work of Sigmund Freud* (Harmondsworth: Penguin 1961), p.220. In Freud's Studies in Hysteria, the 'sexual instinct' is described as the most 'powerful source of lasting increases in excitation (and, as such, of the neuroses).' (as quoted in Jones, p.225).
[2] St. Augustine, *Confessions*, translated by Henry Chadwick, (Oxford: Oxford University Press 1998), p.26.
[3] Ibid., p.145.

population is trying to cope on less than two dollars a day, it might seem odd that our views on sexuality matter so much.[4] Yet it clearly does. All the mainline churches are deeply divided on this issue. The worldwide Anglican Communion is in turmoil because of the election to the episcopacy of an openly gay man in New Hampshire in 2003. Tempting though it is to 'trivialize' the sexual, we need to recognize that Augustine and Freud had a point. Indeed one key assumption I am making in this lecture is that the sexual realm is enormously important. In terms of ethical depth, a person appropriately disciplined in his or her sexual life is likely to be appropriately balanced in other areas of their life. Conversely, a person undisciplined in this area is likely to have problems in other areas of their life. Although global warming and poverty deserve to have a greater priority in our discourse and concerns, it is important not to underestimate the importance of the sexual in our ethical reflection.

Building on this assumption, the argument of this lecture is this. The majority of trends around the sexual in modern western society are disturbing. Divorce and adultery are increasingly commonplace. The internet is a resource for unhealthy sexual addictions. Marriages are finding it difficult to survive the challenges of urban life and mobility. However, one counter balance, however, is the 'gay marriage' debate. This movement for monogamy amongst gay and lesbian couples is a welcome antidote to the disturbing trends. Whereas polyamory continues to undermine monogamy, gay marriage is bringing a mechanism that can support monogamy amongst the homosexual community. Therefore orthodox Christians should be supporting this development. I will conclude my lecture by suggesting that such Christians should own and affirm the designation advocates of 'open orthodoxy'.

Contemporary Culture and Sex

I want to start our discussion about contemporary culture and sex by revisiting the work of the British ethicist V. A. Demant, who wrote in

---

[4] For the poverty statistic see:
http://www.globalissues.org/TradeRelated/Facts.asp#fact1 (accessed Jan 18, 2007)

the 1960s. He observed how difficult the traditional moral life is in a mobile urban culture. Demant believed that virtue is best supported in small, rural communities. With the edifice of modernity, we create a situation where virtue is extremely difficult. If you had to summarize Demant in a slogan, then 'go green for virtue' would be a good one.

Demant makes this argument in his Christian Sex Ethics, where he identifies three main reasons for the sexual obsession of the twentieth century. The first is that

> people are unknowingly driven to venereal experience, and hope for a great sense of fulfillment in it, as a refuge from or compensation for a sense of deprivation elsewhere. The crudest form of this is just a resort to sexual activity as a kind of narcotic... And sex is an even more cogent relief from the pain of individuality and its problems. It is commonplace that sexual desires arise not from natural passion for union with one of the opposite sex, but from a demand to escape from anxiety, however, temporarily. Economic anxieties, worries about esteem and status, intolerable personal relations, hating one's work or despising it, general feelings of failure or cowardice – all this sort of anxiety can be momentarily shed in the sexual embrace.[5]

For Demant, it is so exhausting living in our highly competitive, individualist culture that we seek solace in sexual promiscuity.

The second reason is that our culture has made the demands of marriage difficult to sustain. Demant writes, 'I pointed out that in marriage one is dethroned from a position of superiority and has to live together with husband and wife as equals – all defenses and disguises are down; all masks are stripped off. To anyone with a painful feeling of inner poverty in himself or herself this is a great trial. And when men are given little significance in monotonous work, are easily replaceable and have no sense of responsible citizenship or powers of skill, then they expect tributes to their significance beyond what they earn as a human

---

[5] V. A. Demant, *Christian Sex Ethics*, (London: Hodder and Stoughton 1963), p.116

Courtesy of Shireen Baker

being. Not getting it in the family, as indeed they should not, sexual irregularity is a great temptation.'[6] In a culture where a woodcarver would create a beautiful chair that woodcarver has the self-esteem to cope with the demands of marital intimacy; however, in a culture, where you are on a factory line, self-esteem has been eroded by the work making marital intimacy much harder.

The third reason sums up the first two. Demant writes:

> Sexual adventure outside the bonds of marriage is sought after, mostly quite unconsciously, as a counterweight to the rackets of modern life. . . . There is no home for the soul. However much egoism and emulation enter into sexual adventure, sexual intercourse does penetrate to the biological and pre-conscious level, and even when least enriched by personal affection, it provides moments of intimacy and tenderness.[7]

Demant's view is that urban, mechanical, atomized society with a predominantly intellectual culture, without robust communities and without much contact with nature, starves the emotional life elsewhere. Therefore, argues Demant, too much emotional capital is locked up in the love and marriage relationship which finds it hard to bear the weight. This pressure has led to the situation where people continue to get married but find it difficult to remain faithful and committed.

Combine our cultural obsession with ample opportunity then we have a lethal mix. Demant makes this point repeatedly.[8] The city is a major resource for sexual infidelity. No one can really govern a city. All forms

---

[6] Ibid., p116.
[7] Ibid. p.120.
[8] See, for example, Demant's *Religion and the Decline of Capitalism*.

of human life exist in the city. Unlike the small town, where everyone knows everyone, and nothing 'goes on' without the whole town knowing, the city is completely anonymous. The size of the city means that there is always someone ready to satisfy a need. If one is sufficiently careful, then one can do anything without detection in the city.

Opportunity is also assisted by mobility. If you live in one place, work in another, and are required to travel, then there are ample opportunities to have a liaison with a work colleague or connect for an evening with a stranger you meet in the bar.

I start with Demant because he is one of the few commentators who locates the challenge of fidelity very firmly in the challenge of living in the modern world. Even if both the city and modernity bring many advantages, one can still concede that they make monogamy difficult.[9] And the statistics provides ample evidence for this.

In terms of living arrangements for couples in the United States, only 49% of women in 2005 are living with a spouse at home (53% of men).[10] Back in 1995, 43% of marriages end in divorce or separation within the first fifteen years and this trend has continued.[11] Relationships outside a marriage are harder to determine. Inevitably, such data is shrouded in secrecy. However, in 2002, the best estimates showed that 45-55% of married women and 50-60% of married men have, at some time, had a relationship outside marriage.[12]

Demant could not have foreseen the additional help provided by the internet. Hours can be spent in a chat room or looking at pornography in

---

[9] Also I would want to take issue with Demant's nostalgia for pre-modern forms of work. On the type of work within modernity, Demant is preoccupied with the factory. Fortunately, there are plenty of forms of employment in modernity, which do cultivate self-esteem.

[10] Statistics are for the United States and are taken from the Census Bureau. This statistic is taken from the *New York Times* January 16 2007.

[11] National Center for Health Statistics. Taken from www.divorcereform.org (accessed January 15 2007).

[12] See Joan D. Atwood and Limor Schwartz MA, 'Cyber-Sex' in *Journal of Couple & Relationship Therapy*, 1 (3): 37-56.

the privacy of one's home. Specialists are now talking about the 'cyber-infidelity', which is an 'infidelity that consists of taking energy of any sort (thoughts, feelings and behaviors) outside of the committed relationship in such a way that it damages interactions between the couple and negatively impacts the intimacy in the relationship.'[13] Much like the regular affair, the participants in a cyber-affair offer each other unconditional support and comfort.[14] In addition, 'this electronic bond can offer the fantasy of the excitement, romance and passion that may be missing in the current relationship.'[15] As with the traditional infidelity, the affair starts with 'flirting' (which is often no more than cyber-space chatting), moves to 'cyber-sex' (frequenting the sex chat rooms and engaging in 'sexually explicit cyber talk'[16]) and then allowing it to develop into an affair, which is defined as 'when one partner shares an emotional connection with one participating cyber-friend on the Internet.'[17]

The Internet provides all the temptations of the city. It is a vast, global community. One can meet everyone and anyone from the security of your home. Google can introduce you to someone who shares your particular fantasy. It is not surprising that the Internet has proved to be the pedophile's paradise. With a low risk of being discovered (although fortunately not as low as some child predators would like), one can move from website to website accumulating information on a whole variety of ways of being sexual beings.

In many ways, the polyamory movement makes more sense of our historic moment than the campaign for gay marriage.[18] With mobility and the emergence of urban life, humans have more opportunities than ever before to explore options. One aspect of this is the growing number

---

[13] See Joan D. Atwood and Limor Schwartz MA, 'Cyber-Sex' in *Journal of Couple & Relationship Therapy*, 1 (3): 37-56.
[14] Ibid., p.39.
[15] Ibid., p.39.
[16] Ibid., p.41.
[17] Ibid., p.42.
[18] I have taken this discussion from my book *Do Morals Matter* (Oxford: Blackwell 2007).

of people who simply 'fall in love' with others outside a committed monogamous relationship. For most individuals, this is an affair, but for some this evolves into something more. It could be argued that for the bisexual wife, the loving female companion need not be a threat to the relationship with her husband. There is growing evidence that the affair is evolving into a committed relationship. And this committed relationship is being tolerated by the spouse. And so a polyamorous relationship comes into being.

Churches are beginning to have to face the issue. The Unitarian Universalists are leading the way. This growing US denomination has taken consistently progressive positions on key social issues. So a society has formed – the Unitarian Universalists for Polyamorous Awareness (UUPA). At the 41st General Assembly of the Unitarian Universalists Association, held in 2002, the UUPA succeeded in becoming affiliate member of the Association. The UUPA explains polyamory in the following way:

> Polyamory is the potential for loving more than one person within a given period of time. Here we'll define "love" as a serious, intimate, romantic, stable, affectionate bond which a person has with another person or group of people. Responsible non-monogamy is another way of saying polyamory, and it is used to distinguish polyamory from "cheating."
>
> Polyamory is a general term covering a wide variety of relationship styles, including group marriage (polyfidelity), open marriage, expanded family, intimate network, and some kinds of intentional community.
>
> Polyamory is a relationship choice available to people of any sexual orientation.
>
> Sometimes language familiar to lesbian, gay, bisexual, and transgender people is used to describe aspects of living as a polyamorous person (such as "coming out" as polyamorous). However, there are polyamorous people of all sexual

orientations, just as there are monogamous people of all sexual orientations.[19]

As with all such campaigns, there is a social justice dimension. When it comes to placing children, the US courts have been inclined to view with suspicion households where there are 'irregular' relationships amongst the adults. So the 'poly' welcoming individual wants the law to recognize the legitimacy of this lifestyle choice. This evolving movement has learned much from the gay and lesbian campaign. When the UUPA offers some practical tips for poly welcoming individuals, the website explains that one should:

> Say "partner or partners" instead of "couple."
> Support multiple-person commitment ceremonies.
> Ask a poly person about his or her life. Ask about the person's partner(s) as a way of affirming the importance of those relationships.
> Speak up if someone reveals an irrational fear of polyamory. Be aware of subtle and institutional forms of discrimination against polyamorous people.
> If polyamory brings up strong negative emotions for you, gently explore those feelings by talking with someone you trust.[20]

The cultural pressures on monogamy are considerable. To argue that we should offer our sexual being in the context of a committed relationship sounds positively quaint. So as we start to reflect theologically on same-sex marriage, perhaps the place to begin is around the whole issue of monogamy in general.

Thinking Theologically about Same-Sex Marriage

There are two main arguments for marriage in the Christian tradition. The first is the Roman Catholic argument from Natural Law. Grounded in Aristotle and expressed most fully in the writings of Thomas Aquinas, this starts with the simple observation that children are born of

---

[19] Taken from the website for the UUPA at http://www.uupa.org/Understanding.htm.
[20] Ibid.

parents. Leaving aside the dramatic technological developments that create new and different options, the traditional mechanism of procreation is one man and one woman in the act of sexual intimacy. Given that children, hopefully, outlive their parents, the birth of a child is an obligation that extends for a lifetime. So, the basic God intended unit is the family: one man and one woman in a monogamous relationship for life. Or as the Catechism of the Catholic Church puts it: 'The family is the original cell of social life. It is the natural society in which husband and wife are called to give themselves in love and in the gift of life.'[21] A monogamous committed relationship is the best framework for the rearing of children.

The second argument is Biblical and grounded in the creation story. When it comes to the family, the Bible is an odd text. Many different forms of family are recognized in the text, from polygamy to concubines. And as Deirdre Good has shown, the 'family values' of Jesus are very surprising.[22] Historically, the two texts that most Christians have made central to the marriage debate are Mark 10 (Jesus and divorce) and Genesis 1-3. In Mark 10, Jesus goes back to the creation ordinances. When asked whether divorce, as permitted in the Torah, is appropriate, he goes back to that which God originally intended.

> But Jesus said to them, 'Because of your hardness of heart he wrote this commandment for you. 6 But from the beginning of creation, "God made them male and female." 7"For this reason a man shall leave his father and mother and be joined to his wife, 8and the two shall become one flesh." (Mark 10:5-8)

From Luther onwards, this has been interpreted as Jesus citing the creation ordinance that required one man to marry one woman for their lifetime. And from the Genesis story, one learns that God created male and female to be companions together (Genesis 2:18).

---

[21] The Catechism of the Catholic Church, (Mahwah, N.J., Paulist Press 1994), paragraph 2207, p.533.
[22] See Deirdre Good, Jesus' Family Values, (Church Publishing 2006).

Courtesy of Susan Shillinglaw

Now traditionally, these two texts have been interpreted as the basis for heterosexual monogamy (i.e. marriage). So we come to the issue of 'same-sex' marriage. For many Christians, the natural law argument for heterosexual marriage coupled with the small cluster of passages in the Bible that seem disapproving of homosexuality have settled the question. So, for the Roman Catholic Catechism, homosexual acts 'are contrary to the natural law. They close the sexual act to the gift of life. They do not proceed from a genuine, affective and sexual complementarity. Under no circumstances can they be approved.'[23]

Plenty of others have analyzed the Biblical texts at length. So, in brief, the challenge for the Christian is to think through the attitude of the Biblical witness to 'orientation'. In much the same way as the Bible does not explicitly address 'stem-cell research' or 'nuclear deterrent', so the Bible does not explicitly address our growing awareness that there are significant numbers of people who do choose their sexuality but find themselves living with a certain attraction. It is very difficult to move from the extraordinary story of Sodom, involving attempted gang rape of men and the offer of virgin daughters as a substitute, to a prohibition of a stable gay loving relationship (see Genesis 19). In the Holiness code of Leviticus, we find the prohibition of homosexuality (Leviticus 18:22 and 20:13) sitting alongside the death penalty for adultery and for 'reviling' your mother and father (Leviticus 20:9-10), let alone the requirement that we do not wear a garment with 'two kinds of yarn' (Leviticus 19:19). Consistency would require the Christian who takes one verse from the Holiness Code to take them all (or at least explain

---

[23] The Catechism of the Catholic Church, paragraph 2357, p.566.

why some are binding and others are not.) My sense is that this text is a call for moral distinctiveness from those around us, which is after all the overall purpose of the holiness code; the fundamental settled orientation of a gay and lesbian person is not an issue here. Paul includes homosexuals in the 'vice lists' that occur in several passages of the New Testament, of which the most important is Romans 1. But as with Jesus' propensity to go for dramatic exaggeration (after all most of us look at others with lust in our eyes, but hardly anyone is blind),[24] so Paul denounces experimental homosexual acts by heterosexuals (after all these are men who 'exchanged natural intercourse for unnatural')[25] along with those who are 'rebellious towards parents' who 'deserve to die'.[26] As Richard Burridge has argued these vice lists cannot be the last word on the Christian attitude to rebellious children or homosexuality.[27]

If the texts that convey disapproval of homosexuality are not a decisive Biblical account of sexual orientation, then what about the teaching around creation ordinances in Mark and Genesis? It is interesting to see how a fixed account of marriage has been deduced from Mark 10 rather than the more fluid picture of marriage one might learn from the reply Jesus gives to the Sadducees about the problem of endless remarriages at the resurrection. Jesus says, 'For in the resurrection they neither marry nor are given in marriage, but are like angels in heaven.' (Matthew 22:30) For Jesus, the institution of marriage is a provision intended in this world: it is a temporary institution. Unlike Muslims, Christians do not believe we are married for eternity. And we already recognize that there are countless legitimate marriages, which do not have children: the infertile couple, the elderly couple, and, increasingly, those who do not have children out of choice. And there are those very special marriages which adopt children. The couple creates a family for the child.

---

[24] See Matthew 5:29.
[25] Romans 1:26.
[26] Romans 1:30-32.
[27] See Richard Burridge's forthcoming book.

Most Christians would want to affirm totally the legitimacy of these families. It is disturbing to read Gilbert Meilander's argument that adopted children in families are less legitimate than biological children. Of course, all that Meilander is doing is taking the Natural Law argument extremely seriously and arriving at the logical conclusion that not only is homosexuality problematic but adopted children are as well. Herein is a clue. If the Christian family is flexible enough to incorporate adoption, then perhaps it can be sufficiently flexible to incorporate the gay couple.

Surely the point of a Christian marriage is that two people can create a foundation from which one can provide mutual support and comfort in an ever-changing and often very volatile world. Living in society is difficult to cope with: redundancy might occur at work or a natural disaster might destroy one's home. Although nothing is immune from the transitory nature of being (and of course even one's companion will finally die), there are aspects of one's life which should be more settled than others. The institution of marriage should be a rock on which lives can be lived. As we cope with illness, job insecurity, and anxiety about events in the world, we find at the center of our lives a relationship which provides love through the uncertainty. The point of the narrative in Genesis 2 is that as Adam named all the animals in quest for companion, none of the animals are suitable. It is the contrast between animals and humans which is emphasized. Much as we might like to imagine that the dog or the cat can be a sufficient companion, the point of the Genesis story is that ideally the companion should be human. It is not the gender difference which is central to the story but the necessity that the companion be another human rather than an animal.

The argument for monogamy is that it is the binding commitment of two people that can create the bond sufficiently strong to endure the vicissitudes of life. It is also the setting for sexual intimacy. Augustine and Freud have a point: the sexual realm is complex, powerful, and often dark. Placing sexual intimacy in a setting of trust is the best way of both affirming its significance and satisfying the human sexual need. Open marriages do not work. Polygamy and polyamory have complex power relationships at work within the group, which are almost bound to result in jealousy and insecurity. The point of a marriage is that one should feel 'secure'; to be aware that one is in semi-competition with others for affection and attention is bound to lead to insecurity.

The challenge for the Christian witness at this moment is to witness to the importance of monogamy, while being appropriately pastorally sensitive. There are marriages which are disasters from the moment they start; there are abusive marriages; and marriages being destroyed by some addiction. It is right and proper that people escape from the marriage that becomes a damaging prison. It is also right that the Church makes clear that individuals who find themselves divorced need to know that the grace of God is available for a clean start. But to those individuals who are in adulterous affairs[28] or are tempted by polyamory, the Church needs to be clear. The fruits of the marriage depend on attention to that marriage. Living through the moods and various forms of mid-life crisis, while remaining faithful, is an important part of a marriage.

The paradox of modern living is that we need a monogamous relationship even more. Demant is right to document the ways in which monogamy is difficult in the modern world. But the very fact that many of us are mobile, and that families are now dispersed around a country and the world, makes the need for a center that can provide some form of security even more imperative. The challenge of coping with the demands of modernity requires the committed certainty of a marriage.

The Church is right then to witness to marriage as the appropriate setting for sexual intimacy. We already affirm and celebrate the relationships of the elderly couple – perhaps a widower and widow – and those with special needs, and those whose cross includes the pain of infertility. We are right to affirm and celebrate such marriages. And the time has now come when the same spirit should be extended to the

---

[28] I do acknowledge that there are times when the friendship outside the marriage is partly a result of the marriage relationship being damaging.

committed gay or lesbian couple. If marriage is a good thing, then let us have even more of it.

The Church really should have no problem with the accommodation of same-sex relationships within the marriage institution. Indeed one could argue that perhaps it is more surprising that there is so much demand for monogamous marriage. There are plenty of gay and lesbian thinkers who are strongly opposed to the campaign for same-sex marriage. For Elizabeth Stuart, the Roman Catholic lesbian theologian, marriage has historically served the interests of patriarchy. Instead of emulating heterosexual institutions, she invites the gay community to witness to the alternative. Gay and lesbian people, she argues, have a clearer sense that friendship can blur with sexual desire and are comfortable with the emergence of sexual friendships. She believes that heterosexuals should learn about the connections between love, friendship, and sexual intimacy from the homosexual lifestyle.[29]

Courtesy of Susan Shillinglaw

The Church needs to be clear. For a whole host of reasons, a committed loving relationship between two people is to be commended as part of God's design and intention for creation. The closeness and commitment provide the stability that can help us cope with the demands of modern living. When we make our marriage vows, we commit to making a particular person a priority. Within a marriage, each person matters more than anything else. Yet the marriage is not supposed to form a wall. By providing that secure center, it should facilitate service in the community. Supporting others who are in need is one of the duties of a married couple.

---

[29] See Elizabeth Stuart, *Just Good Friends*, (Lincoln: Andrew Mowbray, 1996).

This affirmation of monogamous marriage is not intended to denigrate the state of singleness. For some, singleness is a preference: for others it is a trial. The natural state for all people is community. And the single person can bring a special gift to community that those in a committed monogamous relationship cannot. Singleness means a greater flexibility and independence that marriage curtails. Not everyone should get married and those who are single can make a special contribution.

An Open Orthodoxy

There is no mention of homosexuality in our Gospels or in the Creeds. Our position on this question should not be the defining credential for orthodoxy or a basis for schism. It is undoubtedly a second order issue. Whereas the concept of God as triune is central to Christian identity, the variety of relationships that the institution of marriage can accommodate is not. Those who have made this central to the identity of Christianity have completely misunderstood the tradition of Christianity.

Orthodoxy involves two affirmations: first, recognition that the Eternal Word was present in the life, death, and resurrection of Jesus. For Christians, we know what God is like by looking at that life. It is the life of Jesus of Nazareth which is the Christian equivalent of the Qur'an. And in understanding that mystery, the Church determined rightly that we need to understand God as a Trinity (there are three aspects within the life of God). The second affirmation is the recognition that the process of the tradition is dynamic, changing, and engaging. If one studies the great theologians of the Christian tradition, then one finds a remarkable dynamic process at work. Augustine of Hippo starts his faith journey by learning from the neoplatonists (followers of that non-Christian who lived many years before Christ called Plato). His faith understanding is a remarkable synthesis of the best of non-Christian thought combined with the discoveries made in Christ. St. Thomas Aquinas in the 13th century does the same work. He is trained as an Augustinian Platonist, yet translated Aristotle and read and engaged with Muslims and Jews. Granted Aquinas is able to combine this hospitality and generosity to Muslims with a vicious critique of the

Qur'an and the Prophet. Yet the process of the tradition is clear: we are called to think afresh within each generation and listen with care to what the Spirit is saying.

Orthodoxy is not a matter of taking the prejudices of the past and imposing them on the present. Orthodoxy is a matter of listening to the revelation of God disclosed in Christ and prayerfully thinking through the implications of our faith for the present. We do so in conversation with the best of non-Christian thought. And from modern science, we learn about orientation. We learn that some people, often at considerable personal distress and pain, have an attraction to persons of the same sex. The orthodox Christian should affirm these insights and accommodate these insights into our ethics of sexuality.

Orthodoxy is not a matter of accommodating every fashion and trend. We cannot and should not affirm every sexual relationship between consenting adults. We should challenge the movement for polyamory. Put positively, we should witness to the importance of monogamy. Orthodox Christians should welcome the gays and lesbians to the institution. The time has come for the gift of monogamy to be shared.

The Christian tradition is generous, hospitable and open. As we struggle with this issue, we should return to the process within our tradition and create for our moment the appropriate understanding of how God expects us to be. Open orthodoxy wants to challenge the extremes. Against John Shelby Spong, justice issues do not require a repudiation of our tradition. Against Peter Akinola, the Christian tradition does not teach that homosexuality is the key issue for communion. Instead, this lecture is an exercise in engaging with the tradition, seeking to be true to that tradition, and therefore demonstrating that the key issue for Christians is that we continue to witness to the importance of monogamy. In that respect, the campaign for same-sex marriage and civil unions is a campaign that orthodox Christians should support. It is in fact a countercultural movement that is challenging many of the more disturbing trends in our society. Instead of opposing the movement, the Church should be standing side by side with those supporters of marriage. While heterosexuals are indulging in infidelity (both cyber and real), we find an important witness to monogamy from our gay and lesbian brothers and sisters. As gays and lesbians ask to be let into the institution, those of us who are already on the inside should reflect and pray on the privilege of marriage and take our duties within the marriage much more seriously.

The Lebel Lectures on Christian Ethics given at University of Calgary, Canada.

Chapter 9

Learning from Radical Orthodoxy: Challenging Sociological Assumptions

A convention accepted by most academics is that you don't talk about topics outside your subject area. Indeed most of us are nervous about commenting on matters outside our immediate area of specialism within our subject. The reason for this convention is our respect for expertise. The journalist or the popularizer is the person who is willing to offer views about everything: the academic recognizes an educational obligation to make sure that one is sufficiently informed before offering a judgment.

So when a book is written by a theologian explaining that a different discipline is an anti-Christian activity and should be strongly resisted by the Church, the temptation is to 'shake one's head' about the impertinent violation of this important convention and assume that it is so ill-informed that it doesn't deserve attention. John Milbank is that theologian. And, on the whole, the vast majority of sociologists of religion have succumbed to this temptation. John Milbank's work has attracted considerable attention elsewhere,[1] but sociologists – with a small number of notable exceptions - have ignored it.[2]

My task in this paper is to attempt to rectify this state of affairs. It will start with a brief survey of Milbank's main arguments as found in *Theology and Social Theory*. It will follow with an analysis of these arguments which suggests that it is true that sociologists do tend to relegate religious explanations for the activities they are studying.

---

[1] The case could be made that amongst English theologians John Milbank is probably the best known. This is in part due to the interest and support of Stanley Hauerwas.
[2] There is some discussion of Milbank's arguments by sociologists, of which the best example is Kieran Flanagan 'Sociology and Milbank's City of God', *in New Blackfrairs*, Vol. 73 No. 861, June 1992, pp. 333-41. Reprinted in Robin Gill (ed) *Theology and Sociology. A Reader* (London: Cassell 1996). But apart from this, the discussion is limited.

However, I shall conclude by showing that this is not a result of sociologists accepting the secular 'ontology of power', but simply sharing a post-Enlightenment propensity to find it difficult to weave together the religious (providential) narratives with the secular ones.

Milbank's *Theology and Social Theory*

To understand this rather dense and difficult tome, one needs to disentangle two major assumptions underpinning his work. The first is his postmodern sympathy with the tradition-constituted nature of rationality (to use Alasdair MacIntyre's famous phrase).[3] And his second is his sympathy with the concept of 'Christian sociology', which was developed by the Christendom group in England in the 1930s.

Dealing with his epistemology first. Milbank takes a distinctive position in the 'truth' debate. We are all familiar with the great divide between the 'non-realists' and the 'critical realists'. Non-realists (sometimes called 'cultural relativists', 'Wittgensteinian fideists', 'Rortyian pragmatists, historicists or postmodernists)[4] stress the 'tradition-constituted' framework that is imposed on our 'sense experience' and the impossibility of determining whether a particular tradition has the correct description of the world. Critical Realists (variously called 'advocates of a correspondence theory of truth', pre-moderns, or in the scientific form 'moderns')[5] concede that interpretation of data is an important part of the knowing process, but insist it is still possible to 'describe the world in better or worse ways'. The issue that divides these two groups is the significance of the tradition of interpretation in the knowing process. For the former, it is decisive: all knowledge claims are filtered through the language and

---

[3] See Alasdair MacIntyre, *Whose Justice? Which Rationality?* (London: Duckworth 1988)
[4] For cultural relativism, Denis Nineham's book *The Use and the Abuse of the Bible* is a good introduction; for Wittgensteinian fideists, the work of D. Z. Phillips is helpful (see his *Faith after Foundationalism*), and for Richard Rorty see *Philosophy and the Mirror of Nature*. For 'historicism' this is the language of John Milbank himself, when attacking the realist instincts of Alasdair MacIntyre in *Whose Justice? Which Rationality?* For postmodernism, see Graham Ward (ed.) *The Postmodern God: A Theological Reader* (Oxford Blackwell 1997) Non-realism is a term associated with the work of Don Cupitt. See, for example, his *Taking Leave of God* (London: SCM Press).
[5] For a good defence of critical realism, see Michael Devitt, *Realism and Truth*.

rationality of the community; for the latter, it is a factor that needs to be taken seriously, but by using the imagination and learning the languages of other communities, it can be transcended. The problem for the non-realists is, if the 'truth' is inaccessible, then surely this makes the quest for the truth redundant and implies we should surrender to the Nietzschian assertion of power. The problem for the realists is that it is not easy to circumvent our locatedness in knowing, which seems to be a condition for any universal 'truth claim'.

Milbank suggests the following alternative: it is true that all we have is a range of different traditions, and decisions between traditions cannot be made on some 'tradition-transcendent' grounds. Yet, it is possible that one of these traditions is the truth. This is what the Christian narrative claims to be: it is a meta-discourse which can and should embrace all human life and activity. Milbank describes this position as 'a true Christian metanarrative realism.'[6] The confident assertion of the Christian narrative can save us from nihilism and violence. 'Such a Christian logic is not deconstructible by modern secular reason; rather, it is Christianity which exposes the non-necessity of supposing, like the Nietzscheans, that difference, non-totalization and indeterminacy of meaning necessarily imply arbitrariness and violence.'[7] So because Milbank's position is post-modern and historicist, he has protected the Christian narrative from secular objections. But because the narrative is true, he has protected himself against the criticism of nihilism.

The second assumption is Milbank's respect for the Christendom Group. For some nine years, John Milbank served as the Reckitt Fellow at the University of Lancaster. It is to his credit that he decided to respect the conditions of the endowment and engage with the Christendom approach. The Christendom group was a movement that started in 1922 (after *The Return of Christendom*[8] was published) and collapsed in the late 1950s (at least the journal ceased to publish). Its most significant member was T. S. Eliot and its most significant

---

[6] J. Milbank, *Theology and Social Theory*, p. 389.
[7] Ibid., p. 5.
[8] See C. Gore introduced, *The Return of Christendom*, By a group of Churchmen (London 1922)

theologian was V. A. Demant (wrongly identified in Milbank's introduction as V. C. Demant). Milbank takes from Demant the idea of 'Christian sociology'.

In Demant's case, natural law was the basis of Christian Sociology. According to Demant, 'The Christian religion provides such a criterion for placing the different activities of man (sic) in their instrumental order, for it has a doctrine of the essential nature of man.'[9] Sociology is an attempt to examine and describe society. Christians with their natural-law insights can offer certain facts about human life which will assist any description of society. Therefore, a Christian sociology will apply Christian natural-law insights together with the sociological methodology. No longer, argued Demant, should we attempt to recommend what 'ought to be', but rather we should be analyzing 'what is'. The church can provide an accurate analysis of the human predicament, not simply platitudes or exhortations for moral improvement.[10]

In an exchange with the English social ethicist, Ronald Preston, John Milbank explicitly invokes Demant and explains: 'he [i.e. Preston] is right to think that I admire the ability of Demant *et al* to call into question certain assumptions of secular power and knowledge (e.g. absolute state sovereignty), however historically well-entrenched they may be, and to ask whether they are really compatible with Christianity.'[11] John Milbank thinks that the category 'Christian Sociology' is a useful one. He explains:

> Talk of 'a Christian sociology' or a 'theology as a social science' is not, therefore, as silly as talk of 'Christian mathematics' (I suspend judgement here) precisely because there can be no sociology in the sense of a universal 'rational' account of the 'social' character of all societies, and Christian sociology is distinctive simply because it explicates, and adopts

---

[9] V. A. Demant, *God, Man, and Society* (London: SCM Press 1933), p. 42.
[10] For a further discussion of Demant's 'Christian Sociology' see my *Plurality and Christian Ethics* (Cambridge: Cambridge University Press 1996) pp.32-34.
[11] John Milbank, 'A Socialist Economic Order' in *Theology* September 1988 p.413-4.

the vantage point of, a distinct society, the Church. But the claim here is not that theology, conceived in a broadly traditional fashion, can now add to its competence certain new, "social" pronouncements. On the contrary, the claim is that all theology has to reconceive itself as a kind of "Christian Sociology": that is to say, as the explication of a socio-linguistic practice or as the constant re-narration of this practice as it has historically developed. The task of such a theology is not apologetics, nor even argument. Rather it is tell again the Christian *mythos*, pronounce again the Christian *logos*, and call again for Christian *praxis* in a manner that restores their freshness and originality. It must articulate Christian difference in such a fashion to make it strange.[12]

So for Milbank, in a marked development of Demant, the concept Christian sociology has two features: first, it emerges from the Church; it reflects Christian thinking: and second, it is all-embracing; it is the telling and living of the Christian drama.

With these two assumptions in mind, we can now turn to *Theology and Social Theory*. Milbank's task in this book is to deconstruct modernity. It is a history, which exposes the hidden assumptions of modernity. Fegus Kerr summarizes Milbank's historical argument thus:

> Historically, according to Milbank, in seventeenth-century thinkers such as Grotius and Hobbes, the concepts of sovereignty, autonomy, property, power, and so on, which were to generate the new "secular" disciplines of political theory, economics and sociology, emerged from the late medieval theological matrix of an effectively non-Trinitarian theism which celebrated a notion of the absolute will of the divine monarch. The "anthropology" which celebrates human beings as atomistic individuals, with their individuality defined essentially as will, would thus be the spin-off of a (distinctly non-Thomist!) voluntarist monotheism. The modern liberal-

---

[12] John Milbank, *Theology and Social Theory*, p.381.

individualist conception of the human person would thus be a product of a heretical (because barely if at all Trinitarian) conception of God.[13]

Catagories, such as 'individual', 'social', 'secular', have a particular history which is a 'theological' history. We have a metaphysics of society here: individuals became the fundamental unit (a construct separated out from any family or community obligations); this created space for the 'social' (which is an entity that transcends individuals); and running parallel with the 'social' is the secular (which is a space made up of non-religious activities), thereby pushing religion entirely to the margins. The whole discourse is a politics that seeks to exclude the religious, thereby making space for human totalitarian forces to occupy the vacuum.

The net result is that the social sciences are exposed as manipulators of power. The secular, on which the social sciences are parasitic, 'had to be invented as the space of "pure power."'[14] Therefore disciplines such as 'sociology of religion' ought to disappear because 'secular reason claims that there is a "social" vantage point from which it can locate and survey various "religious" phenomena. But it has turned out that the assumptions about the nature of religion themselves help to define the perspective of this social vantage.'[15] Sociology has no privilege over theology: insofar as sociology can continue, writes Milbank, 'it would have to redefine itself as a "faith."'[16]

Having deconstructed secularism, Milbank then constructs an account of Christianity as 'a true Christian metanarrative realism.'[17] This, he believes, is the only response to Nietzschian nihilism. Following Augustine's two cities, we now have a cosmic contrast. Christianity is located in a community – the Church – and, unlike the secular, which is built on an ontology of violence, the Church is committed to an

---

[13] Fergus Kerr, *'Simplicity Itself: Milbank's thesis'* reprinted in Robin Gill (ed.) *Theology and Sociology* p.432.
[14] Ibid. p.12.
[15] Ibid. p.139.
[16] Ibid. p. 139.
[17] Ibid. p. 389.

ontology of peace. He concludes the book: [T]he absolute Christian vision of ontological peace now provides the only alternative to a nihilistic outlook.'[18]

His treatment of sociology of religion occurs in chapter five. He makes it clear that his target here is the entire discipline – in all its forms – as it has developed in the west. So he writes, 'I am going to show how all twentieth-century sociology of religion can be exposed as a secular policing of the sublime. Deconstructed in his fashion, the entire subject evaporates into the pure ether of the secular will-to-power.'[19] When he discusses 'American sociology', he outlines the broad picture of religion that emerges in the literature. First, there is the level of private experience; here religion is universal and 'a permanent dimension of human being.'[20] The second level is the particular religious communities where religion is lived and described. Here the 'cultural sub-systems' are seen as 'plural and diverse, reflecting various arbitrary symbolic conventions.'[21] The third level is society. Here, thanks to 'civil religion', it is 'once again universal, because at this level only, symbolic arbitrariness is a cipher for something real, namely, an organic whole, a self-contained system able to conserve its energies in a self-adjusting equilibrium.'[22] Religion is located at the margins and excluded from the middle. So Milbank concludes: 'American sociology therefore reveals that, as a secular policing, its secret purpose is to ensure that religion is kept, conceptually, at the margins – both denied influence, and yet acclaimed for its transcendent purity. . . . What is refused here is the idea that religion might enter into the most basic

Courtesy of Shireen Baker

---

[18] Ibid. p.434.
[19] Ibid. p.106.
[20] Ibid. p. 109.
[21] Ibid.
[22] Ibid.

level of the symbolic organization of society, and the most basic level of its operations of discipline and persuasion, such that one would be unable to abstract a "society" behind and beneath "religion."'[23]

So what is the substance of the Milbank criticism? It seems to be this: academic sociologists of religion are a community that denies its community nature. They are working in a post-Enlightenment framework, which assumes the 'secular' as a neutral vantage point to construct narratives about religion. The historical narrative of the secular is grounded in a heretical theology. The theoretical frameworks, which sociologists use, are opposed to the religious frameworks of the traditions that they are analyzing. And these theoretical frameworks assume that the issues are 'control', 'organization', and 'social influence', instead of 'God', 'the Holy Spirit', and the 'power of prayer'. The former is assuming 'power' as the key to understanding, while the church assumes 'peace' is the key to understanding. So sociologists of religion are not only dishonest (or perhaps to be kinder ignorant), but also working in a framework that is fundamentally unchristian.

Critique of Milbank

One problem with Milbank is that his project operates on so many different levels that it is difficult to know where one starts. Elsewhere, I have raised questions about his epistemology;[24] Kieran Flanagan has raised difficulties with some of the details of his narrative, for example his treatment of Weber and Berger. Others have complained about the 'idealized' church operating in his theology,[25] and his propensity to lapse into vast generalizations about 'all sociology of religion' is problematic.

Turning now to the achievements of his book, many modern sociologists would concede that Milbank is right to attack the positivist assumptions that pervaded some of the pioneering attempts to formulate

---

[23] Ibid.
[24] See Ian Markham *Truth and the Reality of God*.
[25] See Rowan Williams.

a 'sociology of religion'. And the same sociologists are working hard to arrive at narratives that are free from such positivism. Robert Bellah made the point back in 1976, when he distinguished between 'symbolic reductionism' and 'symbolic realism'. Symbolic reductionism seeks to explain religion away, and shaped the work of Marx, Freud, and Durkheim, while 'symbolic realism' does not do this. Symbolic realism is the world of non-objective symbols, which 'express reality and are not reducible to empirical propositions.'[26] (Milbank would note the location of these non-objective symbols and insist that this is still making religion marginal). My focus, however, is on the relationship of the sociological and theological 'discourses': I want to examine Milbank's intuition that sociologists are talking about Christian organizations in a fundamentally anti-christian way.

To do this, I shall explore two ecclesiological illustrations: the first is the Roman Catholic view of Church; the second is a sectarian small church. There is, I want to suggest, some force in the objection that sociologists tend to treat as basically irrelevant the theological narrative that religious communities would provide to justify their actions and intentions. Now at this point, I invoke the convention outlined at the start of my paper: my knowledge of the literature in Sociology of Religion is limited. My expertise is in theology with an interest in the sociological approach. So I do welcome counter-illustrations to my argument.

Consider this description of the Church taken from the Roman Catholic Catechism:

> 752. "In Christian usage, the word 'church' designates the liturgical assembly,[Cf. 1 Cor 11:18 ; 1 Cor 14:19, 28, 34, 35 .] but also the local community[Cf. 1 Cor 1:2 ; 1 Cor 16:1 .] or the whole universal community of believers.[Cf. 1 Cor 15:9 ; Gal 1:13 ; Phil 3:6 .] These three meanings are inseparable. 'The Church' is the People that God gathers in the whole world. She exists in local communities and is made real as a liturgical,

---

[26] See Robert Bellah (ed.) *The New Religious Consciousness* p.351.

above all a Eucharistic, assembly. She draws her life from the word and the body of Christ and so herself becomes Christ's Body."

Courtesy of Rhonda Baker

Sociologists might recognize the liturgical, local and universal aspects of Church; but the metaphysical description that follows would be more problematic, especially the assertion that 'she draws her life from the word and the body of Christ and so herself becomes Christ's Body'. This description of the Church is grounded in Scripture and shaped by the Tradition. Underpinning this description is a theology that believes in the God who is creating a community through Christ to participate in God's action in the world.

Compare this with the way that sociologists use the term 'church' or 'congregation'. Driven by a need to be inclusive of interfaith organizations, Ram Cnaan writes, 'the term "congregation" is used to comprehend church, synagogue, mosque, ashram, and other organized faith-based groups.'[27]

Now it might be objected surely these are just different aspects of the same phenomena? The sociologist is dealing with the social phenomena in the world, while the catechism is capturing the metaphysical reality. The problem with this picture is that the descriptions are *making different assumptions about the world*. The language of 'human organization' when applied to the Church can so often deny the reality of God and the significance of prayer. It assumes a space where God is not present. It concedes the possibility of descriptions that are not theological. It is like saying an altar at a front

---

[27] Ram A. Cnaan, *The Other Philelphia Story,* as found on www.hirr.hartsem.edu.

of a church is a type of table. It is true that there is an ostensible similarity between the shape of an altar and a table in your house, but the dissimilarities are much greater. You eat a meal off the table at home; you can play games around it; you can climb on top of it. It is multi-functional. You should bow before an altar; and it has one primarily purpose, namely the celebration of the Eucharist. The sacred is necessarily part of the description; to treat the altar as part of a wider 'set' of tables is to impose on the altar a discourse that is fundamentally alien to its character. So in the same way to see the Church as just another organization is to deny the truth of the metaphysics, which are the terms in which the Church understands itself.

Some sociologists come close to admitting this.[28] But before developing this discussion, let us turn to my second illustration. Here I compare my reasons for belonging to a small church with the reasons that Carl Dudley, the congregational studies specialist at Hartford Seminary, sets out in his remarkable and delightful classic *Effective Small Churches in the Twenty-first century*. (I am using the revised edition of his 1978 text). Allow me to stress that Dudley's text is intended to be illustrative of a problem; of its type, I think the Dudley book is excellent and in so far as I find fault with it, it is a fault that is almost 'universal' in the discipline of sociology of religion. With these preliminary remarks out of the way, I shall now develop the comparison.

When I was a teenager I belong to a small fundamentalist church in the westcountry of England (Bodmin, Cornwall to be precise). It was ostensibly 'Open Brethren', albeit not very open, and called itself 'Bodmin New Testament Church' (BNTC). The total membership was probably no more than 30 adults and on a Sunday evening at the 'Gospel Service' the congregation rarely exceeded 50 people.

Now we knew we were small; and we had a whole host of explanations for our size. First, we took comfort from the Biblical theme of a

---

[28] Mady A. Thung, 'An Alternative Model for a missionary church: An approach of the Sociology of Religion', in R. Gill ed. p.340-1.

'faithful remnant'. Our Church was small; however we knew that this was God's way of working. Second, we knew these were the end times and one of the signs of the End was that the majority of Churches would be in a state of apostasy. We were sure that the larger and more successful churches in the region had 'compromised' the Gospel. We suspected that other churches were full of 'nominal Christians', who were in desperate need of salvation and certainly were not models for our church. Third, we believed in Satan and believed that Satan was especially active in Bodmin. It was a barren ground because many human lives were consciously enslaved to Satan and hostile to the good news of the Gospel.

Now when I read Carl Dudley's *Effective Small Churches in the Twenty-First Century* none of my reasons I listed for my church being small are considered. Instead Dudley works with a model of a small church that I don't recognize. The small church for Dudley is one where people are attracted to the order (the same people meet up week after week) and to the family intimacy (everyone knows everyone else).

On order, Dudley explains, 'The experience of belonging to a small congregation meets a basic human need for social order and metaphysical orderliness. . . . In the small congregation, the rhythm of the week begins and ends with everything and every person to be found in his or her rightful place.'[29] Now this is perhaps a factor for some (after all, he does cite the FACT data – a point I shall come to in a moment), however in my case there was no 'metaphysical orderliness'. Indeed the theological explanation for the size of the congregation was not due to 'metaphysical order' but disorder: it was the exact opposite. The size of BNTC was due to the state of human sinfulness and the surrounding antagonism to God. It was a matter of personal sadness that the vast majority of people I passed as I walked to Church on a Sunday morning were on the way to hell and that they are not in their 'rightful' place in Church.

---

[29] Carl Dudley, *Effective Small Churches in the Twenty-first century*, (Nashville: Abingdon Press 2003) p.43.

On family intimacy, Dudley spends several chapters reflecting on the problem of 'family intimacy' and church growth. Dudley assumes that all churches want to grow and therefore the dilemma is how best to grow while preserving the intimacy of the community. He suggests the model of 'adoption' – one he notes that is firmly grounded in the Bible: so he writes, 'Adoption should be a part of church growth . . . The purpose of "adoption" is to help the pride in a congregation's Christian record become the common property of the congregation, not the private possession of a few.'[30] Now Dudley is right that this small church did have a family intimacy; it is also true that anyone joining the church rapidly became part of the family. However, the problem I have here is that social analysis is the organizing paradigm for the understanding the way faith is expressed in small church. BNTC would find the preoccupation with 'social analysis' odd (bit like an altar being compared to a table), the Bible is what matters. Furthermore BNTC would not talk about the problem of Church growth simply as one of integration into the community. Our strongly Calvinist sympathies meant that we left God to do the recruiting, and 'church growth' for 'church growth's sake was a value of the world.[31] We on theological grounds disapproved of big churches: they had almost certainly surrendered (or compromised – a much favored word) the Gospel. Our job was to be faithful and if God was going to bless our Church that that is up to God. Although Dudley has captured two aspects of the small church (family intimacy and adoption as the model for new members), he has done so while misunderstanding the underlying dispositions that shape our attitude to those outside and therefore our underlying disposition to growth.

At this point three objections might be raised. The first is that Dudley has data that supports his arguments. The second is that this is not a clash between sociologist and theologian, but between different types of theology. Dudley's theology is liberal and positive, while BNTC is sectarian and closed. The third objection is that this is no more than a

---

[30] Ibid. p.66-7.
[31] Dudley does recognize that despite some of their leaders, many small churches do not want to grow.

plea for the James Hopewell approach to congregational studies; one that takes the 'identity' of a congregation seriously. I shall deal with each of these objections in turn.

It is true that Dudley has considerable data that supports his assertions that the family intimacy of the church is a major attraction for that Church. But Milbank's response would be to point out that Dudley asks the questions. The sociologists take their non-theological framework in which they pose the questions and then treat this as evidence for their explanations. In BNTC explanations for our internal life is grounded in a Biblical worldview that believes in a cosmic battle between God and Satan, which will culminate in an imminent end to the world.

In respect to the second objection, again it is true that Dudley works hard to develop a theological and biblical rationale to better understand the small church embodiment of their shared faith. But my point is that the social analysis is prior, the theology is second. The type of theology is irrelevant; it is the status in the discourse.

This leads to the third and most substantive objection. James F. Hopewell's now classic study *Congregation: Stories and Structures* is clearly preoccupied with the need to understand the theological narrative that shapes a faith community. He divides approaches to congregational studies into four: contextual (i.e. the immediate environment), mechanical (the functional aspects), organic (the biographic aspect), and symbolic (the identity). Hopewell argues for the symbolic approach. He writes,

> The approach considers the congregation less a texture or machine or organism than a discourse, an exchange of symbols that express the views, values, and motivations of the parish. . . .[T]he symbolic outlook . . . focuses upon its identity. Identity mirrors the "we" of a church that persists through whatever changes environment or revised program or interpersonal growth may effect in its midst. Throughout such changes any congregation remains itself, irrepressibly recognizable to its members and other observers. The marks and patterns of that

recognition are the symbols this fourth approach seeks to discover.[32]

To discover the worldview of a congregation, Hopewell offers a variety of tools, including a participant observation, guided interviews, and 'A World View' test instrument. Congregational studies, explains Hopewell, needs to take seriously the beliefs and stories that underpin a congregation.

The difficulty with Hopewell's approach is this: he is collecting further data for the sociologist to 'explain'; he is not inviting the congregation to 'explain' the data themselves. Naturally, good sociologists are interested in a community's narrative; but this narrative is relocated into a sociological framework as a piece that then requires further sociological analysis.

Perhaps the problem is captured by David Martin when he wrote: 'A sociologist has no remit to talk about God. If he were to talk directly about God he would immediately convert himself into a theologian or a philosopher of history or a prophet. To speak of God in the world is an act of unveiling. . . It is no business of the sociologist to distinguish the true and lively word from any other statement.'[33] Martin has his own distinctive attempt to solve this conumdrum, however, for now I want to stay with the problem.

Take almost any debate in Sociology of Religion, we will find similar narrative conflicts. Growing Churches, to oversimplify the complex literature, are largely suburban, middle class, and conservative. Growing Churches, according to the Christians inside them, are ones that are praying and as a result being transformed by the action of the Holy Spirit. European religion explains Grace Davie, (again oversimplifying a complex book)[34] is in a process of mutation; partly due to the problem of 'gathering' in Europe, religious institutions have fewer

---

[32] James F. Hopewell, *Congregation: Stories and Structures*, edited by Barbara Wheeler, (Philadelphia: Fortress Press 1987) p.28-9.
[33] David Martin *The Breaking of the Image* (Oxford Blackwell 1980).
[34] See Grace Davie, *Religion in Europe: A Memory Mutates* (Oxford: Oxford University Press 2000).

congregants, but religious dispositions are continuing in a variety of different ways. European religion, explains many African Christians, is in a state of sin and rebellion against God due to a consumerist attitude and increasing secular unbelief. It seems then that Milbank does have a point: sociological narratives seem to be incompatible with religious ones.

Locating the Debate

For sociologists of religion, there are two aspects to the Milbank challenge. The first can be accommodated fairly easily. It would be worthwhile to collect rather more data on the **explanations** that the 'subjects' in any enquiry would give for their predicament. In other words offer the data to the community and listen to their theological explanation for that data. Often, as we have seen, this does appear in the descriptive part of the sociological study; but these religious accounts then disappear as the sociologists provides their own 'expert' explanation for 'what is really going on'. And the legitimacy of this process leads us to the second aspect of Milbank's challenge.

The second aspect is one that is found in a range of disciplines. For many years, fundamentalist Biblical scholars have complained about the 'presuppositions' of the critical study of the Bible. And William Abrahams raised an extremely sophisticated version of this challenge in two excellent books published in the early 1980s. Abrahams raises the question whether the exegetical assumptions made by biblical scholars about this or that miracle are simply the 'reading into the text' the assumptions of modernity. If God is really active, then there is no reason at all why the resurrection might not have occurred. One should not assume that these features of the text need to be 'explained away' because our modern age has not encountered many resurrected people.

Biblical studies has also had to struggle with the problem of providence and history. The 8th century prophetic interpretation for the fall of Judah in 587BCE is that God was judging the Jewish people for their failure to be faithful to the covenant. The historian's account tends to assume it is the regular regional problem of small nations and large empires. The explanation is political not religious.

Courtesy of Rhonda Baker

The science and religion debate has had to grapple with a comparable issue. In the Scriptures, God is the agent directly responsible for the weather: in our modern period we tend to treat the weather as a self-generating system, which is in large matter predictable. At one point, if at all, does God intervene?

Providing an account of providence that harmonizes with the historical, sociological, and scientific narratives of modernity continues to be a difficult for modern theology. Some opt for levels of explanation: this is the strategy of the physicists John Polkinghorne. If you wanted an explanation for this lecture, then a computer read out of my brain activity during this lecture would be one level. However, few would consider this a total explanation. And another level of explanation would be in terms of human intention and therefore a summary of my argument. So by analogy the sociological, historical, and scientific levels of explanation are opting at the same level as the computer print out. Another strategy is the route taken by Austin Farrer – double agency. The God explanation and the sociological, historical and scientific narrative are really one and the same. In retrospect one can see the theological narrative, which at the time one simply interpreted sociologically. Precisely how these two narratives merge is, explains Farrer, a mystery. But it is precisely the 'eye of faith' that sees this merger.

It is not my purpose in this paper to solve this conundrum. In one sense seeing how widespread the problem of reconciling narratives mitigates the Milbank challenge. He is simply stating in a new way an old problem. And perhaps the problem is easier to solve than we often imagine. Allow me in conclusion to introduce you to the worldview of my seven year old. It is his birthday. Mysterious presents from England have been arriving all week. On the morning of his birthday, he marches into the bedroom – where my wife and I are sleeping – passes the big pile of wrapped presents by the door and continues on to the bathroom to relieve himself. As he does so, we distinctly hear him remark: 'Thank you God and thank you all my relatives in England'. Quite so, Luke Markham, the sociological and theological narratives reconciled through the eyes of faith.

Chapter 10

Spirituality Meets Civic Engagement

Abstract: This paper starts with David Hay's data about the vast increase over the last n people in the UK having religious experiences. This data confirms the underlying religious dispositions of the British, although there is clearly a significant decline of participation in religious institutions. However, as many have noted, religious organizations are amongst the strongest in civic society (more in church than involved in political parties). So we need to tap into the spiritual motivation to encourage a range of participation in civic society from boy scouts to Rotary. The American sociologist Nancy Ammerman has shown that the more a person is involved in one organization the more they end up being involved in lots of organizations. Therefore spirituality is an important basis for civic engagement.

For some at Leeds Met, the theme of spirituality meeting civic engagement may sound odd. It will be odd on two levels. First, the word 'spirituality' sounds 'other-worldly' and preoccupied with the sense of the divine. One does not expect the word to be linked with the practical and 'this worldly'. Spirituality being linked to civic engagement sounds like MacDonald's being linked to a low chlorestrol diet – it looks like a stretch. Second, for those who believe that Richard Dawkins – Britain's professional atheist – anticipates the future, it is puzzling why we are still bothering with religion at all. The default secularism in British society, where congregations are getting smaller and increasingly composed of the elderly, leads the realm of the spiritual looking irrelevant.

Drawing on the insights learned from the social sciences – (a strength here at Leeds Met), this lecture will argue that both of these perceptions are mistaken. The argument will show that spirituality and religious belief in Britain are strong. However, civic engagement is weak (and this includes participation in congregations). Interestingly, those who are involved in congregations are more likely to be involved in civic society. Then drawing on theology, I shall demonstrate that this sociological reality is also confirmed by theology – it is right and proper that an interest in God extends to an interest in humanity and community.

The Religious Disposition of the British

There is no disputing the significant decline in congregational participation. Unlike some of the traditional explanations for secularism (where religious decline was linked to modernity and science), the sociologist Steve Bruce attributes the decline to 'indifference'. Steve Bruce writes:

> 'We may want to explain the secularity of some elite groups (such as professional scientists) by the impact of science and rationalism, but to understand the mass of the population it is not self-conscious irreligion that is important. It is indifference. The primary cause of indifference is the lack of religious socialization and the lack of constant background affirmation of beliefs.'[1]

There is a cultural shift at work here which no longer takes religious catagories seriously.

Two scholars who take issue with Steve Bruce is Grace Davie and David Hay. Grace Davie has documented the ways in which religious life in Europe seems to be 'mutating' but not disappearing. Grace Davie writes:

> For particular historical reasons (notably the historic connections between Church and State), significant numbers of Europeans are content to let both churches and churchgoers enact a memory on their behalf (the essential meaning of vicarious), more than

---

[1] Steve Bruce, *God is Dead: Secularization in the West*, (Oxford: Blackwell 2002) p.240.

half aware that they might need to draw on the capital at crucial times in their individual or their collective lives. The almost universal take up of religious ceremonies at the time of death is the most obvious expression of this tendency; so, too, the prominence of the historic churches in particular at times of national crisis or, more positively, of national celebration. Think, for example, of the significance of European churches and church buildings after the sinking of the Baltic ferry *Estonia*, after the death of Princess Diana or after the terrifying events of 11 September 2001.[2]

Countries with a church tax system continue to collect revenue, even if the donors do not actually attend. And when a crisis erupts, argues Davie, churches are suddenly 'used' as a mechanism of coping with the trauma. Although this might not be a particularly demanding form of religious life, it is still very much there. It is undoubtedly true that modernity has not created thousands of atheists and agnostics. Scratch a European you will find underneath the apparent indifferent exterior, a person interested in 'new age' and 'spirituality'. The few atheists and agnostics assume that most of their friends are just like them. This is not true. The world is full of people of faith.

David Hay's work confirms this analysis. David Hay is an educationalist, who is deeply interested in religious experience. In his recent study *Something there: the biology of the human spirit*, he starts by explaining a key assumption. He writes: 'I am a committed Darwinian, but …I am [also] a religious believer.'[3] The first step for Hay is to draw attention to the significant numbers of people who report that they have an awareness of God. In 1987 almost half of the population of the Britain reported a spiritual experience. 29% talked about seeing God in the 'patterning of events' around them; 27% had an awareness of the presence of God; and 25% had moments when prayer

---

[2] Grace Davie, *Europe: The Exceptional Case. Parameters of Faith in the Modern World* (London: Darton, Longman and Todd 2002) p.19.
[3] David Hay, *Something There: The Biology of the Human Spirit*, (West Conshohocken, PA: Templeton Foundation Press 2006), p.xi.

was answered.[4] Now the most extraordinary finding is that the same questions were asked in 2000. Followers of Richard Dawkins would have expected a significant decline. However, as Hay writes, 'I was astonished when I received the results. ... Over those 13 years there had been an almost 60 per cent increase in the positive response rate. The figures suggest that around three quarters of the national population are now likely to admit to having had one of these experiences. The great majority of these people are of course not regular churchgoers.'[5] So 55% see God in the patterning of events, 38% have an awareness of God, and 37% have an awareness of answered prayer.

The second step for Hay is to build on the work of his mentor Alister Hardy. Hay summarizes the work of Hardy thus:

> Hardy expressed his conviction that all of us as members of the species *Homo sapiens* have the potential for spiritual awareness. Amongst the thousands of metaphors human beings have used to describe it we might say: a presence rolling through all things, an unnamed power, God or the gods, a power coming from the unconscious, or ... energy drawn from the earth itself. Hardy argued that this awareness is like a sense; it is there because it has an important function. It has indeed been "naturally selected" in the process of evolution because it helps us to survive.[6]

For Hardy, we are – to use a phrase found elsewhere – we are religious animals. At some point in our evolutionary history, we had experiences of the 'divine' that we distinguished from everyday experiences. And indeed there is evidence for this sort of sensitivity reaching back some 60,000 years into our human evolutionary history. Now of course, we might invoke the arguments of Karl Marx or Sigmund Freud or Emile Durkheim as an explanation for this data: the problem is that the scientific data does not support this. People who experience the divine are often middle class (rather than poor as Marx would expect); they are

---

[4] Ibid. p.11.
[5] Ibid. p.9.
[6] Ibid. p.37.

often experiences which contrast sharply with our experience of our parents (*contra* Freud); and they are often counter-cultural (*contra* Durkheim). For Hay, the biological truth about humanity is that we have a 'spiritual sense' – a sense analogous with our other senses. And in situations where British people are invited to talk about these experiences, most have them.

So the British continue to be religious, albeit differently so from the past. They are having experiences of the transcendent and continue to affirm some reality beyond this world. They are also happy to allow a small minority to represent them in congregations. People who live in small villages around England want the church to remain open; they want services to be held; they want the church there when they need it; and they are pleased that a small minority are doing the hard work of keeping their church operational on their behalf.

We can go further. The truth about the British is that the challenges facing the congregation extend beyond the congregation. Anything that requires people to join and organize is struggling. Civic society in Britain is in trouble.

The crisis facing civic society[7]

The European Values Survey is a remarkable tool. If we think Churches are in trouble, then it is worth comparing them with other groups and organizations in society. The data is interesting.

This first chart is the league table of belonging in Great Britain:

Belong to none	65.9%
Belong to education, arts, music, or cultural activities	9.7%

---

[7] Much of the data for this section comes from The European Values Survey for 2000. Found at http://www.jdsurvey.net/web/evs1.htm (accessed Nov 25 2008)

Belong to labor unions	8.2%
Belong to social welfare service for elderly	6.7%
Belong to youth work	5.7%
Belong to other groups	5.1%
Belong to religious organizations	5%
Belong to local political actions	3.8%
Belong to sports or recreation	3%
Belong to organization concerned with health	3%
Belong to voluntary organization and activity linked to third world development or human rights	2.7%
Belong to Political Party	2.5%
Belong to a women's group	1.7%
Belong to a professional association	1.6%

Belong to conservation, the environment, ecology and animal rights	1.5%
Belong to peace movement	0.6%

According to this data, it looks as if religious organizations are holding up relatively well. Compared to membership of political parties or sports related organizations, churches are congregations are strong. Yet the most shocking aspect of the data is that almost 66% of the population do not belong to anything.

Interestingly, a higher percentage of the population are involved in some sort of volunteer work; youth work, health related, and social welfare attract the highest numbers. As this chart demonstrates.

The second chart documents unpaid work. The following emerges:

Unpaid work none	56.9%
Unpaid Youth Work	15.3%
Unpaid work social welfare service for elderly, handicapped or deprived people	13.4%
Unpaid work organization concerned with health	10%

Unpaid work professional associations	7.8%
Unpaid work environment, conservation, animal rights	7.8%
Unpaid work religious or church organization	6.3%
Unpaid work human rights	4.3%
Unpaid work peace movement	4.3%
Unpaid work sports or recreation	4%
Unpaid work education, arts, music, or cultural activities	2.8%
Unpaid work labor unions	2.3%
Unpaid work political parties or groups	1.4%
Unpaid work women's group	1.3%

However, two conclusions stand out. The first is that volunteer activity in churches and religious organizations remains strong. And the second is that it attracts many more volunteers than political parties, trade unions, or other social justice causes.

Grace Davie is right to stress the similarities between religious organizations and other organizations. She explains that insofar as the churches need to reorganize themselves radically, 'it must also be so for a whole range of other institutions which struggle for organizational existence in modern Europe. It is quite clear, for instance, that churches are not the only institutions which have lost members in the post-war period and which now seek alternative forms of organization. Obvious examples of this situation can be found in the political parties and in the associations of organized labor.'[8]

The conclusion we should draw is that the British are finding it increasingly difficult to belong to anything. The mixture of high quality home entertainment, individuals opting to create small informal networks, and a consumerism which resents the effort of organization has destroyed the layer of organizations between the individual and the state (what the conservative political theorist Edmund Burke called the 'little platoon'). Most people do not belong to anything. It is not as if people have stopped going to churches and are now involved in community organizations, rather people have stopped going to anything. In between the individual and the state, the layer of 'organizations' is disappearing – what the conservative political theorist Edmund Burke called 'the little platoons' have gone. Although we might belong to a gym, we do not belong to anything that requires effort and organization. We don't want to be the Treasurer of a society.

So why exactly is this? I am yet to find the British equivalent of Robert Putnam's classic *Bowling Alone*. This is a study of 'social capital' in the United States. Although social capital is much stronger than anything you find in Europe, Putnam notes that there has been a significant decline in the last third of the twentieth century. People now 'bowl alone' rather than in groups. He identifies four reasons for this decline, which are probably true of the UK as well. Putnam explains:

---

[8] Grace Davie, *Religion in Modern Europe: A Memory Mutates*, p.50

> First, pressures of time and money, including the special pressures on two-career families, contributed measurely to the diminution of our social and community involvement during these years. . . . Second, suburbanization, communting, and sprawl also played a supporting role. . . Third, the effect of electronic entertainment – above all, television – in privatizing our leisure time has been substantial. . . .Fourth and most important, generational change – the slow, steady, and ineluctable replacement of the long civic generation by their less involved children and grandchildren – has been a very powerful factor.[9]

So the likeliest explanation, which I think can also be applied to Britain, is the following: civic engagement became harder as our lifestyle required two-career families, commutes became longer, high quality home entertainment increasingly available, and as a membership generation was replaced by generations interested in small informal networks.

Now does this matter? In my view it does. In *Do Morals Matter?*, I argued that a Morally-Serious Person is one that recognizes a civic responsibility by participating in community related organizations. This is important for several reasons. First, it leads to an enhanced sense of self and community. We are intended to work together. It is a tragic society that simply watches the television, attends an occasional movie, and does not develop deep connections outside the family.

Second, it creates a culture where we enjoy 'generalized reciprocity', which Putnam defines as 'I'll do this for you without expecting anything specific back from you, in the confident expectation that someone else will do something for me down the road.'[10] So when I help out at a 'Soup Kitchen' for the homeless, I don't do it expecting an immediate benefit, rather I serve a culture that is there for others. So Putnam writes, 'A society characterized by generalized reciprocity is

---

[9] Robert Putnam, *Bowling Alone: The Collapse and Revival of American Community*, (New York: Simon & Schuster 2000) p.283
[10] Robert Putnam, *Bowling Alone*, p.21.

more efficient than a distrustful society, for the same reason that money is more efficient than barter. If we don't have to balance every exchange instantly, we can get a lot more accomplished. Trustworthiness lubricates social life. Frequent interaction among a diverse set of people tends to produce a norm of generalized reciprocity.'[11] This flows into the third reason why it matters, which is civic participation supports a vast range of social services and networks that support those in need. The Salvation Army helps the homeless; Scouts help children; and various initiatives for persons with special needs helps the families who otherwise carry the responsibility for care alone. Finally, and perhaps most dramatically, it protects against the dangers of totalitarianism. One of the arguments of Bellah's *et al* classic *Habits of the Hearts* is that an America (in this case) where individuals stop joining organizations is vulnerable to the totalitarian encroachment. An individual cannot stop the abuse of power by the state. However, organizations have real power. An organization means that people are meeting; they can, if need be, be mobilized; and organizations ensure that communication is shared. It is no coincidence that totalitarian rulers seek to undermine any competing organizations that might challenge the state (one of the reasons, of course, for Stalin's brutal attacks on religious organizations).

Tapping into British religious sensitivity can help civic society

Thus far we have seen two contrasting tendencies. The first is that the British remain robustly religious: the second is that the lack of membership of congregations is part of a wider (and in my view more disturbing) trend of organizational disinterest.

I shall now argue that the challenge is to link our religious sensitivities to greater participation in society. The British propensity towards spirituality needs an outlet in congregations and other organizations. Now at this point one might object that participation in a religious congregation is likely to dissipate the wider involvement in society. However, this is not the case. Indeed, as Robin Gill and Nancy

---

[11] Ibid. p.21.

Ammerman have shown, the opposite is true: a person who is involved in a congregation is more likely to be involved in other organizations.

Robin Gill's study draws on the data from the British Household Panel Survey. In this study, Gill explains, 'a very high 27% of members of voluntary service groups reported that they were weekly churchgoers (in the sample as a whole it was 11%) and 42% went at least once a month (it was 18% in the whole sample).'[12] Nancy Ammerman's *Pillars of Faith* demonstrates that persons of faith make much of the voluntary work in America possible. Often this is in a direct way – the congregation has a partner in the community or supports a denominational program committed to social justice; however, it is also in an indirect way – a person of faith simply gets involved in more organizations because of his or her faith commitments.

Nancy Ammerman's work puts to rest an anxiety that a person's involvement in a congregation will make it less likely that he or she is involved in the community. The truth seems to be the opposite. Once a person has managed to leave the home for one evening a week, then it is likely that they will leave the home for two or three evenings a week. In other words, once a person joins one organization (say a congregation) that person is more likely to join another congregation. The secret is to get a person to join at least one organization.

Theological Reflection

The truth discerned by sociologists is confirmed by theology. God wants us involved in our communities. Part of the *Imago Dei* is our capacity to be in relationship with others. Indeed, for the Abrahamic traditions, this is a primary reason why we are created. The universe came to be to enable sophisticated consciousness to emerge that has the capacity to relate to others – to give and receive love.

This essay was originally published in Implicit Religion.

---

[12] Robin Gill, *Churchgoing and Christian Ethics*, (Cambridge: Cambridge University Press 1999), p.106.

Chapter 11

Conversing with Islam: A Visit with the Pat Robertson of Pakistan

The besetting sin of much of the Interfaith Dialogue movement is that it just brings together liberals from each religion. As a result, the outcome of these dialogues is completely predictable. We all sit around and celebrate the fact that we are talking to each other. Then we moan that so many of our co-religionists are not like us.

The problem, we explain to each other, is that our respective fundamentalists view faith in an inflexible and uncompromising way. We need to encourage them, we announce, to be less literal and see doctrine as "myth." The dialogue concludes with the challenge to the participants to make their own conservatives less inflexible and more open. And we all leave feeling smug, confident that we are "where it is at."

The sins are many. Hubris, arrogance and ignorance are the big three. It isn't really dialogue across difference; it is a game of mutually affirming prejudice amongst liberals. And it excludes the vast majority of religious people. Most Christians, Hindus, Jews, Buddhists and Muslims really believe in their traditions; they accept the particularities of their faith. They believe in the infallibility of their holy books.

This exclusion compounds the sins of those of us involved in interfaith dialogue because the task of persuading authentic believers in the various religions to commit to interreligious dialogue is a moral imperative. Although it is unfair to blame all the problems of the world on religion, it is true that religion is not always playing the constructive role it should, and this is partly due to the lack of mutual understanding.

So it was with some pleasure that I accepted an invitation to join a mixed group of Christians and Muslims, with one Jew and one Sikh, to visit Lahore in Pakistan. Dr. Israr Ahmed was our host. It was an opportunity to converse with an authentically traditional form of Islam, albeit one that was idiosyncratic.

Dr. Ahmed has a significant profile in Pakistan. He appears for at least two hours on Qur'an Television every day. He has set forth an Islamic systematic theology in a range of books and videos. Although his movement in Pakistan is small (some 2,000 members), it is clear that there is a wider penumbra of sympathy for his views. He is the Islamic equivalent of Pat Robertson in America; the majority of Christians in North America would not concur with Robertson's worldview, nevertheless he does speak for a significant minority.

He starts from the classical starting points of the infallibility of the Qur'an, the importance of *hadith,* and crucially, for Ahmed, the *Seerah* (biography) of the prophet Muhammad. Although his teaching concerning the nature and content of these sources are found amongst many Islamic teachers, he does offer a number of distinctive positions. He is one of the few Islamic intellectuals to harmonize the Qur'anic text with the narrative of evolution. He accepts the time line of 15 billion years or so and the slow development of species gradually over time. However, he insists on two divine interventions: one at the point when a new species emerges and the other when Neanderthal humanity was given a soul and became a human being. On this question, Ahmed is close to the position known as "theistic evolution." In terms of dialogue, this Christian theologian found it easy to make connections.

It was his social teaching that proved a greater challenge. First, he is an advocate for the traditional role of women. Although in terms of moral status women are considered equal to men, he believes that all women should be married. And within marriage, men and women are unequal; wives must obey their husbands. Outside the home they should wear the burka (i.e. be completely covered). In addition, "free intermixing of the sexes will be (in an Islamic State) prohibited and in principle separate areas of activity will be determined for men and women."

He goes on: "Men and women will have separate educational institutes, hospitals, etc., and the segregation of sexes will be upheld in every facet of social life."[13] The reason for this is that the mixing of the sexes is so damaging. He explains: "Mixed (non-segregated) social living debased the West as far as modesty, chastity and purity are concerned. It destroyed the domestic peace and confounded the family structure."[14]

As a Christian completely persuaded that we have much to learn from feminism, this worldview is a challenge to me. Some Muslim feminists are sympathetic to the argument that the wearing of the veil is helpful in a patriarchal society that treats women as objects of sexual desire and lust. Some lesbian separatists might be sympathetic to the need for the segregation of the sexes, although they wouldn't exactly warm to the obligation to be married.

However, most perhaps would worry about the assumptions underpinning this worldview. Why should men tell women what they are permitted to wear? Given women are required to control their lustful thoughts as they look at the hair of a good looking young man, then why can't men learn to do likewise? However, of course, there is an "authority" issue here; there is a verse in the Qur'an (as of course there is in the New Testament) that encourages the woman be covered. So my arguments for feminism need to recognize the challenge of the Qur'anic text.

Most interesting was Ahmed's call for "revolution" to bring about an Islamic state. On revolution, Ahmed teaches that the democratic processes make too many anti-Islamic assumptions, such that the only way forward is revolution. He writes, "Obviously, these colossal, all embracing and basic changes [e.g., the eradication of interest and the total segregation of the sexes] are not possible by political process and elections because by such process an established system can be run or at best partially improved but cannot be changed. Nor is this possible by

---

[13] Israr Ahmed, *Khilafah in Pakistan. What, Why and How?* (Lahore: Maktaba Markarzi Anjuman Khuddam-ul-Quran 2001) p.8.
[14] Ibid. p.4.

fragmentary and gradual reformation as it can bring about only superficial, not fundamental change. This change can come about through complete revolution for which a revolutionary party is essential."[15]

At this point, Ahmed reminded me of the small groups of Marxists in Britain and America during the 20th century that used to have interminable debates about the best way to bring about a communist society. Stage one, he explained, is passive resistance. The Muslims must disseminate this vision to others and recruit sympathizers. Stage two is active resistance, where the Muslims fight against the excesses of secularism and apply pressure on the system for an alternative vision. Stage three, if necessary, is active aggression. It is the final push to take control of the State, which may require force.

The vision of the State includes much that is predictable: sovereignty belongs to God alone; harsh penalties for serving or consuming alcohol and other drugs; and no laws or political programs can be permitted that are incompatible with the Qur'an and *Sunnah*. Non-Muslims (Christians, Jews, Buddhists, etc.) in the state will have the same rights as Muslims in terms of protection of their lives and property. However, he explains, "In an Islamic State, non-Muslims cannot take part in the highest level of policy making, neither can they participate in the process of legislation."[16] So we cannot vote or lead a political party.

All of this is deeply problematic. Although healthy democracies need the anarchist and Marxist voices that question the fundamentals of the system (and in that sense Ahmed's perspective is a useful one), there are many good reasons for our conviction that a peaceful transition from one vision of the common good to another through the vote of people is a better system than any available alternative. And in a world where the 20th century saw a Civil Rights campaign in the United States to end segregation coupled with the apartheid regime collapsing in South Africa, we do not want to move back to a state that constitutionally

---

[15] Ibid. p.8.
[16] Ibid. p.26.

entrenches the concept of a second-class citizen on the basis of religion. In these respects Ahmed's vision of the world needs to be strongly contested and resisted.

At Hartford Seminary, we have a slogan: "We talk to anyone willing to talk to us." Naturally this means that some will self-select themselves out. However, authentic dialogue must welcome the conservative voices to the table. Unlike the mutually affirming liberal dialogues, these authentic dialogues will be much more uncomfortable, sometimes even offensive. Disagreement will be inevitable. However, it is this sort of dialogue on which the future of the world really does depend. Those who believe in liberal values must be willing to talk to those who have doubts and question those values. In that sense, I appreciated the conversation with Dr. Ahmed very much.

Zion's Herald, March-April 2004. Reprinted by permission of The Progressive Christian, http://www.tpcmagazine.org.

Chapter 12

Is Greed So Bad?

It is easy to give greed a bad rap. Greed has to do with excess and self-indulgence. It looks like a very obvious vice. As we have come to terms with the dramatic economic decline, 'greed' has been blamed. Almost anyone involved in the financial sector (from mortgages to investments) has been characterized as 'greedy'. Greed is the big sin of capitalism, which, according to this worldview, is responsible for the mess we are currently in.

Before we get carried away with this denunciation of greed, we need to pause and allow ourselves to become a little more nuanced. In a world where there is no greed, there would be no desire. A major motivating force for self-improvement would disappear. People innovate, work hard, and pioneer because they want to be a little more comfortable, to have the larger home, to enjoy an IPod and fine wine.

In fact, cases of blatant greed are fairly rare. Those involved in the sub-prime mortgage debacle were more guilty of stupidity than greed. It was stupid to assume that the housing market values in the United States were going to increase at the same dramatic rate; this was not greedy, but stupid. Granted, some greed might be reflected in the desire for a commission by an individual mortgage consultant, but this is a relatively minor factor. Those who invested in Bernard Madoff's Ponzi scheme were not necessarily greedy. The charities that had invested with Madoff wanted to get the best possible return so they could give more away: it is an odd sort of greed that culminates in philanthropy.

The truth is that we are made by God to seek to improve our lot by labor. Any thoughtful account of human agency in this world must recognize that this world requires an aspiration to succeed. Nothing comes easily. We need to toil on the land for food; we need to build if we want shelter. The basics require motivation; and this basic motivation is an aspiration for anything beyond being a nomadic scavenger. We don't survive unless we have some 'greedy' desire.

In other words Michael Novak in *The Spirit of Democratic Capitalism* and Richard John Neuhaus in *Doing Well and Doing Good* had it right. Part of the Image of God is a capacity to create, to work hard, and to succeed. In other words, a basic greedy aspiration is not part of the Fall, but part of the Imago Dei.

Naturally, there does come a point where greed can be destructive. To be a two-car family can be a necessity in modern America, to own sixteen is a wicked misuse of resources. To live life to accumulate more wealth than one can enjoy is sin. Part of the joy of being rewarded appropriately for one's labor is the opportunity to give to others. One should be greedy for both oneself and others.

This is Aristotle's insight. For Aristotle in *The Nicomachean Ethics*, greed is contrasted with generosity. Generosity, argued Aristotle, is the mean between wastefulness and greed. The desire for things is not wrong, but the desire to keep all these things for oneself is. But once this is seen, we can now see why this constant critique that the economic crisis is 'all due to too much greed' is so mistaken. If this were the case, then the failure of the investment bankers and mortgage consultants would be the lack of generosity. But this wasn't the problem. Stupidity was the problem. What we need now is for an intelligent propensity to greed which has generous outcomes. Living in this world is living in a way that God always intended us to live.

This essay was originally published at Patheos.com in 2009.

Chapter 13

Seeing through faith

I once asked a group of Tanzania Christian pastors in Dodoma Tanzania, "Do you ever doubt the truth of Christianity?" Their answer indicated that there was general agreement that "doubt" was an issue, but it took a particular form. For these well-educated, technologically savvy (they all had cell-phones) pastors, doubt does not touch the reality of the religious dimension or the spiritual realm. No one was tempted by scientific reductionism. Instead, in the battle between "spiritism" and "Christianity", they did as pastors sometimes do, doubt the Christian claim that Jesus has the victory over the "principalities and powers". In a world where the "curse" is feared, the strength of Jesus to resist that "curse" is a real issue.

In parts of Europe and some of the urban centers in the United States, "doubt" takes a more regular form. Here the pervasive achievement of science is much more obvious. Here the narrative of the God explanation has over the last four hundred years been steadily undermined by physics, chemistry, and biology (and the concept of providence has been challenged by political science and modern historical methods). For persons in this arena, "doubt" is the sense that the religious realm is a complete illusion.

This difference is well known. It is yet another illustration of the ways in which our setting, immediate history, and conversation partners are such major factors in our worldview. Live in the world of biology, be a member of an Oxford college in an increasingly secular England, it is likely you will look at the world like Richard Dawkins. Live nearer the land, appreciate the vulnerability of being in a Tanzanian village, then it is likely you will look at the world like a syncretistic animist Christian.

Tempting though it is to stop the conversation there, and surrender to relativism, this is not necessary. Instead we are forced to recognize the "rootedness" of knowing. Appreciating different worldviews is hard work; and it requires patient listening and empathy. We are, as Alasdair MacIntyre observed, "tradition-constituted", and yet also able to engage across traditions to grow into a greater appreciation of the truth about the world.

It is interesting how "atheism" has never really caught on. The few who articulate the worldview have the feel of the blind person who cannot appreciate colors. To those inside the faith fold, there is a strange disconnect with experience and the atheistic arguments. And the atheism of Richard Dawkins, Christopher Hitchens, and Sam Harris is especially odd. It is clearly a "middle-class" atheism; it assumes a western worldview. It treats religion as if it is no more than a belief in some sort of add-on object, when faith claims religion in so much more.

There are three problems with this sort of atheism. The first is that the fellow-atheists don't find it convincing. Nietzsche understood the significance of religion in the world. For Nietzsche, once God goes, many other things go. Truth, Nietzsche points out, depends on the intelligibility of the universe; yet once God goes, intelligibility goes, and therefore truth is undermined. For Nietzsche, moral language is clearly grounded in the transcendent, so once the transcendent goes, the moral needs to be redefined. Our trinity of atheists doesn't want to go there: so the implications of atheism are totally ignored.

The second is that the science of our modern day atheists sounds almost metaphysical. This comes out most clearly when Richard Dawkins discusses the debates in astrophysics around the "anthropic principle". Dawkins concedes the data – it is clear that the emergence of life here in this universe is heavily dependent on a multitude of factors that statistically are so completely improbable. Dawkins opts for the skeptical alternative – the multiverse theory. This states that along with this vast universe (and it really is extremely big), there are billions of other universes. Most of these universes do not generate life, but we just happen to be in the one that does. Once upon a time, it was only religious people who believed in more than one universe – this one, heaven, and hell; now atheists have billions upon billions of universes. Given the choice of theism or the multiverse theory for the remarkable math of this universe, the multiverse theory is a stretch and certainly sounds almost "religious".

Courtesy of Susan Shillinglaw

The third is that the nature of faith is not understood. Perhaps this is inevitable because you do have to be inside to know this. Faith is analogous to sight. I completely understand why blind people are skeptical about colors – seeing people disagree about what color is what, the inability for seeing people to explain what colors are exactly, and therefore there is no decisive argument for color. However, those of us who experience colors know that they are there (and granted, philosophically that is a contentious statement). By analogy, the gift of faith is learned. In this respect the disciples of Wittgenstein are right. We learn the language of faith. We learn to see the world through the lens of faith and in so doing, there are countless mutually confirming experiences of faith.

Atheism is an interesting conversation partner for faith. Atheists do serve an important purpose when they draw attention to the hypocrisy and damage that many religions inflict. However, in the end, atheism is probably a less significant conversation partner than the "spiritism" conversation in Tanzania. The future lies with people who can see. The question is how can we interweave the various descriptions of the spiritual realm together?

Originally published at Philosophypress.co.uk in 2010.

Chapter 14

Richard Burridge's Jesus
Imitating Jesus: reading the Eternal Word

For the six years I was at Hartford Seminary (which is one-third Muslim), I had the enjoyable challenge of teaching Christian doctrine to Muslims. I have lost count of the number of conversations I have with Muslims who invite me to compare the Bible and the Qur'an and admit that the Qur'an looks much more like the Word of God than the Bible. In every case, I would push back and insist that they are not comparing like with like. For Christians, the primary Word of God is the Eternal Word – the Word made flesh in the life, death and resurrection of Jesus. In fact, I would explain the right way to compare the Qur'an is not with the Bible but with the Eternal Word made flesh.[1] The incarnation is the Christian equivalent of the Qur'an. And perhaps it is better to see the Bible as closer to the Hadith. At this point, the same question is asked: 'but how is it possible to read a life?'

Richard Burridge has provided the answer. However, before we get to this answer, let us frame out the Christian claim about the location of the definitive Word of God rather more. The Eternal Word is identical with the 'Son' within the Trinity. To oversimplify, and opt for a particular account of, the incarnation, Christians claim that the Eternal Word completely interpenetrates the life, death and resurrection of

---

[1] The other advantage of this comparison is that it helps Muslims to see why the doctrine of the Trinity is necessary for Christians. Muslims believe that the Qur'an as the Word of God must be eternal and have pre-existed the creation. They do this for sound theological reasons: God's Word would not simply start but must have always been with God even in eternity past. If the Eternal Word made flesh is the Christian equivalent of the Qur'an, then one can start to understand why pre-existence of the Son became so important in Christian doctrine. And one can further understand that Christians did not want the Word of God sitting in eternity past separate from the Creator, so the doctrine of the Trinity emerged to safeguard our monotheistic commitments.

Jesus. This is the primary Word, which means that ultimately if you want to know what God is like then you need to read a life. This means that technically we are not people of a book, for the primary Word of God is a life.

Almost everything about the past comes through a text (it is only relatively recently that images – photographs and video – have become available). So given the incarnation is a past event, Christians believe that there is a Written Word which is important. These are the scriptures. However, the precise relationship between the Written Word and the Eternal Word is a matter of considerable debate.

In this response to *Imitating Jesus*, I will form two arguments. First, with *Imitating Jesus*, the debate about the relationship between the Eternal Word and the Written Word has been changed forever. The second is that the one person who doesn't quite see the significance of the argument is the author of *Imitating Jesus*. I shall now unpack these two arguments.

The relationship of the Eternal Word to the Written Word in Imitating Jesus

The argument of *Imitating Jesus* is elegant in its simplicity. It is a Christological argument. First, Burridge explains that the gospels are properly understood as 'biography' or 'ancient lives' (pp. 24–31). Second, the purpose of the gospel is to invite us to imitate the 'words and deeds' of Jesus of Nazareth. Third, the gospels celebrate different aspects of the character, discourse and actions of Jesus, but all exhort 'imitation'. Fourth, the 'words' of Jesus often exhort us to live transformed lives, while the deeds of Jesus witness to a full inclusion of all those who struggle with those exhortations. Fifth, the rest of the New Testament (certainly Paul's epistles) describes a community which affirms both poles of the task of 'imitating Jesus'. Sixth, we are called both to witness to transformed lives and include in the conversation all those who struggle with that work of transformation. Seventh, keeping the community broad is also a way of making sure that the dominant narrative is really committed to the work of faithful transformation.

Courtesy of Susan Shillinglaw

How exactly does this argument shape the theological conversation about the relationship between the Eternal Word and the Written Word? It does so in several ways. The history of Christian ethics has tended to play down the Eternal Word and focus on the Written Word. For those in the Reformed and Lutheran traditions, the role of Jesus was primarily soteriological. The life was played down and the focus was almost entirely on the atonement. The death of Jesus was important for soteriological reasons and the life was a necessary prelude to the death. For those in the Catholic traditions, Aristotelian philosophy would supplement the text of scripture and the disclosure of the Eternal Word was clearly secondary. In both cases, the Bible was important, but Jesus was less so. One reason for this is that the tradition was not entirely clear how to 'read a life'. In addition, the Bible was easier – in the text there is a wealth of ethical instruction and exhortation. Thus the Written Word was the basis for ethical discussion and the Eternal Word was neglected.

Richard Burridge has demonstrated that this relegation of Jesus is gravely misguided. In fact, the opposite is true. To read the New Testament properly one must see the centrality of Jesus. And the whole concept of *bios* (ancient biography) could be interpreted as the way in which one can 'read the Eternal Word' disclosed in the life, death and resurrection of Jesus.

In other words, for Burridge, the intent of the authors in the New Testament (it is lovely to have the concept of authorial intent back in the frame) was to create a community that imitated both the words and deeds of Jesus of Nazareth. Once Jesus was no longer with the disciples, we have the early church working hard to create the tools to continue this task of imitating Jesus.

The result of taking the disclosure of the Eternal Word in Jesus as the control (not that Burridge puts it like this, but this I think is how a theologian should interpret his argument) is striking. We are required by Christ to live within an inclusive community, which does not rush to exclude, even when we think the other is gravely mistaken. It is a call for a conversation around the most exacting standards of holiness within community.

In this book Richard Burridge actually provides an important argument that supports a Barthian approach to scripture. For Barth, there is an important connection between the Word and the text of scripture. For after all, it is the Bible that tells us about the Word, which is Jesus. Karl Barth in *Church Dogmatics* explores at some length precisely what it means to call the Bible the Word of God. Barth explains:

> God is not an attribute of something else, even if this something else is the Bible. God is the Subject, God is Lord. He is Lord even over the Bible and in the Bible. The statement that the Bible is the Word of God cannot therefore say that the Word of God is tied to the Bible. On the contrary, what it must say is that Bible is tied to the Word of God. . . . If the Church lives by the Bible because it is the Word of God, that means that it lives by the fact that Christ is revealed in the Bible by the work of the Holy Spirit.[2]

For Karl Barth, the primary disclosure of God is the Word of God which is the life, death and resurrection of Jesus of Nazareth. For Barth, the Bible becomes the Word as it witnesses to the Word which is Jesus. And the manner in which this occurs is also determined by the Word of God himself. Barth writes:

---

[2] Karl Barth, *Church Dogmatics*, I/2 (Edinburgh: T&T Clark, 1963), p. 513.

> As to when, where and how the Bible shows itself to us in this event as the Word of God, we do not decide, but the Word of God Himself decides, at different times in the Church and with different men confirming and renewing the event of instituting and inspiring the prophets and apostles to be His witnesses and servants, so that in their written word they again live before us, not as men who once spoke in Jerusalem and Samaria, to the Romans and Corinthians, but as men who in all the concreteness of their own situation and action speak to us here and now.[3]

For Barth, there is a Trinitarian dynamic at work between the Word of God, which is Jesus, and the Bible, as the Word of God. The Bible, through the agency of the Holy Spirit, can become an immediate text, confronting a particular moment, with the disclosure of God, which is the Eternal Word (perhaps this also happened in South Africa). With this emphasis on the primary Word as the Eternal Word, which completely interpenetrates the life of Jesus of Nazareth, we can see that our primary obligation is to read a life – a life which was very enigmatic.

So we return to Richard Burridge and the gospels. Our definitive disclosure of what God is like is a poor young man from Nazareth, who took enormous risks as he reached out to include the marginalized – especially women, the poor and the reviled. He found himself a victim of power – finally dying as a common criminal at the hands of the occupying power. Yet remarkably, the movement he birthed believed that death was not able to hold him. Reports of his resurrection started to circulate and so the church was born.

So what do we know about God from the Eternal Word? We know that God is on the side of those who are least fortunate. We know that the love of God is willing to go to any length for the sake of humanity. We know that in our moments of despair God promises to create hope. We

---

[3] Ibid., pp. 530–1.

know that we should treat this life as authoritative. We should imitate the 'words and deeds' of Jesus of Nazareth.

Now our obligation as Christians is to recognise the authority of this life in guiding our witness today. This obligation extends to our interpretation of the rest of the Bible. If the Bible is interpreted in such a way as to contradict what we 'read' from the life, death and resurrection of the Eternal Word, then we have an obligation to revisit the text of the Bible. Although slavery is instituted in Leviticus and condoned in the pastoral epistles, the legitimacy of slavery is clearly incompatible with the disclosure of God in the life, death and resurrection of Jesus.

Reading the Qur'an can be difficult, but reading a life is harder.[4] So Christians are, right from the outset, bound to have to live with a pluralism of positions; hence the importance of the inclusive community. Although the slave traders are outside the zone of acceptable pluralism, there are a multitude of positions with which the life of Jesus might be compatible. The areas of debate include the following: gratuitous war is clearly unacceptable, but the use of force to create a just peace might be acceptable; exploitative capitalism is clearly wrong, but the use of the profit motive to create an effective system of resource allocation might be acceptable; and life should not be created to be destroyed, but the cultivation of stem cells for the advancement of medical techniques that heal genetic diseases might be appropriate. Reading a life does have a major advantage over a text. It permits significant flexibility over time. We are imitating the 'words and deeds' of

Courtesy of Susan Shillinglaw

---

[4] I do of course recognize that reading the Qur'an is difficult. I am very interested in the various ways in which the Qur'an is interpreted, particularly with the emphasis on those verses which have local significance and those which have more universal significance.

Jesus. This exercise starts in the New Testament and we can see how the church struggles to arrive at the appropriate inclusive position over the gentiles and the Jewish law. And so it continues with Augustine and Aquinas.

The movement for Christian thought is to move constantly, to and fro, from the life, death and resurrection of Jesus of Nazareth (as it flows through the sacraments and life of the church) to the particularities of each situation. With the Spirit of God constantly making the Eternal Word present to each situation, we can and should allow our faith to engage with each situation making use of all the resources available to us. The resources flow from our conviction of the threefold nature of God: a creator who creates every single life and loves each particular life and seeks to disclose truth to those lives; a revealer and redeemer who discloses the nature of God (thereby providing a definitive norm) and also redeems all people; and a Spirit who is constantly making God present and allowing us to see God in new and different ways.

On this account, Richard Burridge has provided the New Testament justification for the Barthian view of the relationship between the Eternal Word and the Written Word.

The author's lack of appreciation for his own remarkable argument

Perhaps it is only after one has finished a book that one starts to appreciate the full implications of the argument. It is in the last chapter that Richard starts to relate his argument with the range of traditional approaches to New Testament ethics. So, in his thoughtful chapter on apartheid, he starts by explaining how 'authorial intent' can be problematic (and not a control on what is biblical, p. 353). Then he moves to the opposite extreme 'reader response criticism' (p. 354); then he brings 'the two horizons together' (pp. 356–7) and it is here he engages with the approach of Richard Hays. All these approaches are found wanting because of the lack of appreciation of genre. So Burridge writes, 'We have argued throughout this book that genre is the key to understanding of texts, providing a kind of agreement, often unspoken or even unconscious, between author and audience, to guide their proper interpretation' (p. 360). Burridge is right, genre is the key, but what he overlooks is that it is not simply a literary key, but a theological key.

As he works through the apartheid case study, he examines 'rules and commands' (p. 363), 'principles and universal values' (p. 368), 'examples and paradigms' (p. 376), 'overall symbolic worldview' (p. 382) and 'reading together in an inclusive community' (p. 388). It is this latter approach which Burridge believes emerges from his argument.

However, what he overlooks is that all his approaches are assuming the primacy and centrality of the Written Word. He lacks the recognition that his argument is bringing together the Eternal Word as the control over the interpretation of the Written Word (as an act of fidelity to the approach to ethics taken by the rest of the New Testament). He needed an ethical approach which makes it clear that discerning what God is like from the Eternal Word is the primary responsibility of the Christian and the primary obligation of the Christian faithful to the New Testament witness.

It is an approach which makes sure that all scripture is interpreted through a Christological lens. What Burridge has done is demonstrate that Barth's approach to scripture is in agreement with the message and meaning of the New Testament.

Conclusion

This is a vitally important book. This is a book on which others will want to build. What Christian piety has known for a century – you discover what God requires by looking at Jesus – Burridge has confirmed. What various trajectories of Christian ethical reflection have overlooked, Burridge has corrected. The challenge of learning to read a life, Burridge has illuminated. We should all be grateful to Richard Burridge for this remarkable text.

© *Scottish Journal of Theology. Originally published in Scottish Journal of Theology 63:3 (2010), pp. 340-345. Reprinted with permission.*

Chapter 15

Did Bush Cooperate with Terrorists?
Making conspiracy theories respectable can be dangerous

David Ray Griffin is a distinguished theologian. He is Professor of Philosophy of Religion at Claremont School of Theology. He has written and edited more than 20 books and is one of the country's leading "process" theologians.

His latest book is a significant departure from process theology. It is called *The New Pearl Harbor: Disturbing Questions about the Bush Administration and 9/11*. The argument of the book is that the official version of the World Trade Center and Pentagon attacks is highly implausible. At the very least, Griffin suspects that high level officials constructed a false account, but he also says it is possible that intelligence agencies had prior knowledge of the attacks, or even that the White House might have been involved in the planning of the attacks.

The list of endorsements is impressive. Richard Falk from Princeton writes a glowing forward. Howard Zinn (author of *A People's History of the United States*), John McMurtry (Canadian professor of philosophy), Rosemary Radford Ruether (professor of feminist theology), John Cobb Jr. (professor of theology), and Joseph Hough (president of Union Theological Seminary) all add their tributes to the book.

The argument, explains Griffin, is cumulative; that is, it is an "argument consisting of several particulars that are independent of each other" (p. xxiv). So once the hijacked planes departed from their scheduled routes on 9/11, then proper protocol would have required the military to challenge the planes. This did not happen. The towers should not have collapsed, and the way the towers collapsed is best explained in terms of explosives. It was probably a guided missile that hit the Pentagon, which would explain why there was no debris from the Boeing 757. Add to all this the evidence for warnings that an attack was planned and the strange behavior of the president at the elementary school in Florida, and Griffin feels that he has a strong "prima facie case for official complicity" that requires investigation (p.xxiii).

Courtesy of FEMA

The book was written while the National Commission on Terrorist Attacks was doing its work. Griffin is skeptical that the Commission had the time, resources, or the independence to really get to all the difficult questions. However, *The 9/11 Commission Report* does provide alternative explanations for much of Griffin's data. The reason why military aircraft did not intercept the hijacked flights was partly due to the fact that the protocols for the FAA "requires multiple levels of notification and approval at the highest levels of government"[1] and partly because the FAA did not know where the planes were due to the hijackers turning off the aircraft's transponder.[2] The president's confused reaction was a combination of being misinformed at 8:55 a.m. that a "small, twin-engine plane"[3] had hit the World Trade Center and then a desire to "project calm" as he listened to the children reading.[4] Of course, one can debate whether

---

[1] The 9/11 Commission Report. Final Report of the National Commission on Terrorist Attacks Upon the United States. Authorized edition. p. 17.
[2] Ibid p. 20.
[3] Ibid p. 35. Andrew Card – White House Chief of Staff – was responsible for this piece of misinformation. Condoleezza Rice recalls then adding – in the course of the conversation – that it was a commercial.
[4] Ibid. p.38.

this was the most appropriate response; but it is not evidence that "the White House expected some sort of attack" (p. 64). Indeed the counter argument is equally easy to make: If President Bush did know that the attacks were going to take place he would have planned a different photo op and response. The simplest explanation was that President Bush – like all of us – was in a state of some shock and bewilderment. People in shock do behave in strange ways.

The Commission report does criticize the intelligence agencies. Griffin is right to say that there were signs of an imminent attack. The Commission does not discuss alternative possible explanations for the collapse of the World Trade Towers, although it is clear that the plane in the North Tower did cause a fire ball to travel down the elevator shafts.[5] Also, the report does not question the cause of the Pentagon attack.[6] But perhaps we should not expect the report to consider every hypothesis that has been circulating on the Internet and then given respectability by David Ray Griffin. There needs to be limits to the range of possibilities considered; and I want to suggest that Griffin is outside them.

Let me explain why.

Conspiracy theories abound in every area of life. Apparently, the Roman Catholic Church has tried to keep secret the marriage of Jesus; Proctor and Gamble is under the control of Satanists; and the English establishment had Princess Diana killed because it could not tolerate the idea of the future mother of the King of England having a Muslim husband. A significant factor in all conspiracy theories is a deep bias or antagonism. So, for example, the Holocaust deniers, such as David Irving, produced their heavily referenced works, making the case that Auschwitz had insufficient gas chambers for the numbers that were killed. However, I suspect that David Ray Griffin would join me in not even dignifying the argument with serious consideration because of the

---

[5] Ibid. p.292.
[6] See Ibid. p.314.

deep antagonism that the holocaust deniers have for the Jewish people. We are both confident that the bias has so distorted their worldview that there is little point in disentangling the good arguments from the prejudice.

The antagonism in David Ray Griffin's book is against America. He quotes with approval the journalist Patrick Martin, "In examining any crime, a central question must be 'who benefits?' the principal beneficiaries of the destruction of the World Trade Center are in the United States: the Bush administration, the Pentagon, the CIA and FBI, the weapons industry, the oil industry. It is reasonable to ask whether those who have profited to such an extent from this tragedy contributed to bringing it about" (p.127). Apparently, the ways in which Bush *et al* have benefited include: increased popularity after 9/11, vast increase in military spending, more funding for covert operations, fresh support for the missile defense system and so on.

For the anti-Americans, whatever America does is bad. In 1998, Richard Rubinstein at the American Academy of Religion meeting mused on American inactivity in Kosovo to defend the Muslims. He argued that this is due to the American sympathy with the European vision of a Europe free of the Jew and Muslim. When the bombing started in 1999, Noam Chomsky attacked it as an example of the new imperialism.[7] Both inactivity and activity can be given an anti-American slant. The prejudice asserts itself by searching for a narrative (an interpretation) that connects certain events in an anti-American way. The narratives are always simple. So, for Griffin, before 9/11 Bush was in trouble and afterwards he was able to progress upon his quest for world domination.

In reality the world is much more complicated. It is true that sometimes America makes morally ambiguous decisions – for example, the training of Osama bin Laden to become a tool against the Russian

---

[7] See Noam Chomsky, The New Military Humanism. Lessons from Kosovo (Monroe: Common Courage Press, 1999).

occupation of Afghanistan. It is also true that events change presidents. George Bush campaigned as a person who didn't "believe in nation building." This changed after 9/11. It is also true that intelligence agencies make mistakes; of weapons of mass destruction in Iraq, which the military failed to find. In this fallen world, nations misinform and make mistakes.

But America under Bush is not Hitler's Germany. Such parallels are not justified. It is true that Americans want to be able to trade, import oil, and travel safely; but it is not true that they want to destroy cultures, peoples and dominate nations. America will disentangle from Iraq and hopefully resource the rebuilding of that nation. Social commentary needs to be responsible. When a book argues that the American president deliberately and knowingly was "involved" in the slaughter of 3000 U.S. citizens, then this is irresponsible. We can be sure that Griffin's book will be widely translated and read in countries ready to believe the worst about America. In terms of building cross-cultural understanding, this is a deeply damaging book.

If David Ray Griffin had come to me, I would have refused to endorse the book. I do not think the book should have been written. It feeds a paranoia that is not justified. In so doing, it distorts significantly the legitimate political discourse that should challenge this administration. There are problems with current policy that should be pointed out, but suggesting that Bush cooperated with the terrorists is not one of them.

Zion's Herald, November-December 2004. Reprinted by permission of The Progressive Christian, http://www.tpcmagazine.org.

Postscript

All writing is autobiographical. We reveal more of ourselves than we care to admit in the aside, in the illustration, in the theme, of a sermon or a paper. Periodically, it is a good exercise to make the explicit the autobiographical elements expressed implicitly in a book.

Perhaps a primary theme is the ways in which the tragic can be revelatory of God and redeemed by God. The death of my mother at the age of 17 remains a pivotal experience in my past. The illness was relatively brief. Some ten months from diagnosis to death. It ran parallel with the year when I was retaking my 'A' Levels to get into University (the Advanced Level credential was then the recognized credential for entry into a UK university). I did not behave well as my mother struggled with the illness and finally died. And as I struggled with the loss, I joined the ranks of many before me, who wondered 'why didn't God heal her?' I remember vividly a wise old man gently reprimanding me: 'Didn't you realize Ian before this moment that mothers die leaving children without mothers? Didn't you realize Ian that our Lord dying is at the heart of the Christian drama?'

The tragic is part of and central to the Christian faith. When dealing with a tragedy, such as the burning of a Chapel, one starts and ends with the crucified and resurrected Jesus. Life is always surrounded by tragedy. We live sensitive to our mortality. When we are not adjusting to the loss of someone we love, we live constantly in fear of loss (my wife and I worry constantly about the health and safety of our son). Living with this sensitivity shouldn't make us depressed or excessively anxious. Instead, we should live with a sense of gratitude for the gift of each day of life and vitality. And when the tragic comes, it should not overwhelm us. Instead we are invited to revisit the drama of the cross and resurrection and live anew with the hope that the tragic is never the end but simply a stage to hope.

Such an understanding of the world is necessarily grounded in an orthodox understanding of the Christian drama. This is also a major theme of this book. We live in a time when there is impatience with doctrine. It seems incidental to living. One feature of my journey is an increasing confidence about the Christian drama. And this confidence needs to be located in a certain understanding of the truth.

The truth about living is that all worldviews are provisional. Everything we believe needs to be held with some humility. Complete certainty is not an option. However, one should not move from this sensitivity to an indifferent relativism. The quest for truth is primary. There are worldviews that make more sense of the world than other worldviews. A conspiratorial worldview that suggests that President George W. Bush organized 9/11 is a very implausible worldview. Although one cannot say with complete certainty that it is definitely false, one can say that the evidence for that position is poor and it is very unlikely to be true. An Islamist worldview that seeks to create a segregated society of men and women where minorities are denied their full human rights is deeply misguided at many levels; it denies the discovery of human rights, which are intrinsic to every person by virtue of simply being. Although one cannot say with complete certainty that it is definitely false, one can say that the difficulties with this position are so overwhelming that it should be resisted (and I am pleased to report it is being resisted by many Muslims).

Truth is the human project of seeking to make sense of the complexity of the world in as a coherent and full way as possible. The claim that Jesus is the Incarnate Word is not incoherent. And given Richard Burridge's exposition of New Testament ethics, it is the insight that makes sense of the New Testament. There is evidence that the remarkable phenomenon of Christianity is good evidence for the truth of the Incarnation. However, even here one is not invited to a place of complete certainty. One must acknowledge and live with the possibility of doubt and, very probably, seasons when doubt is very real. This is God-intended doubt. We should not be afraid of such seasons.

This understanding of truth has been a major theme of much of my work. *Truth and the Reality of God*[8] argued for a 'realist' account of truth that took seriously the complexity of discovering that truth. Theologically, the idea here is that God deliberately put humanity in a position where our contingency and limitedness as creatures makes discernment of the truth difficult but not impossible. God wants us to live in community and learn from each other. God wants us to hold our insights with humility and do so in conversation with each other.

From this picture of truth, another theme of the book emerges – the importance of engagement. Engagement is not a betrayal of the Christian tradition, but an obligation of the tradition. As Christians, we need to think through the implications of the tradition for such topics as same-sex marriage and civic society. I am very conscious that this theme of engagement is a reaction to my fundamentalist upbringing. When you grow up in the Exclusive Brethren, one is allergic to forms of Christianity that replicate the Exclusives propensity to withdraw from society and refuse to engage with contemporary culture.

As a result of my commitment to engagement, the work of 'Radical Orthodoxy' has been a problem for me. For a time, I saw an engagement approach as opposed to the Radical Orthodoxy of John Milbank. However, as this volume now concedes the Radical Orthodoxy movement has rightly exposed the dangers of the Church reducing theology to sociology. Christian engagement needs to be on certain terms. Christians do want to come into the conversation with a certain anthropology (one which denies the reductionism of so much of the social sciences) and a certain understanding of the reality and agency of God.

Perhaps this is a good place to conclude this postscript. My admission that my initial reaction to Radical Orthodoxy was mistaken captures in part the approach to theology and faith that I am seeking to commend in this set of sermons and lectures. It is an approach that assumes that God expects us to be revising our understanding of God and God's relations

---

[8] Ian Markham, *Truth and the Reality of God*, (Edinburgh: T&T Clark 1998)

with this world of ours. It is an approach that offers up to God our provisional understandings of God and God's relations with the world. This side of the eschaton, there is no such thing as the 'Last Word'. The work of theology is a shared corporate task. This volume is intended to be one small contribution to an ongoing journey of faith.

- Ian Markham

www.ingramcontent.com/pod-product-compliance
Lightning Source LLC
Chambersburg PA
CBHW071126090426
42736CB00012B/2032